Consent
Is
Morality

A Philosophy of Peace

Sean Leal

Author inquiries contact:
publishing@seanleal.com

Ordering information visit:
ConsentIsMorality.com

Print ISBN: 978-1-71654-469-9

First Edition

To all my Facebook friends who contributed to the conversation:
Thank you

To Lisa:
"Thank you" isn't enough

To my family:
It is to you this is book is dedicated

Preface

You intuitively know that respecting the choices people make is one of the highest values, and that violating someone's consent can sometimes be a horrible or even unforgivable transgression. Deep down, you get the fundamental importance of consent, but you want a deeper understanding. You want some concrete arguments and logic so you can explain to others *why* violating consent is "wrong" in the first place, other than saying, "Well, of *course* it's wrong."

In that case, you need to read this book.

Many other people vastly more intelligent than myself laid the groundwork for nearly everything mentioned herein. For the most part, these people will remain unnamed for a couple of important reasons.

The first reason being, an idea is either true or it is not. Personally, I don't need to know who originally came up with the idea that 2+2=4. The truth of $a^2+b^2=c^2$ is correct whether we call it the Pythagorean Theorem[1] or simply the theorem of right triangles.

Second is an unfortunate attribute of living in an era of social networks, where even the most non-controversial ideas are immediately given a political label, assigned to a "team," then dismissed without examination merely based on *who* said them.

---

[1] https://proofwiki.org/wiki/Pythagoras%27s_Theorem

I prefer that the ideas in this book speak on their own merit and allow the honestly curious reader to explore them and their natural logical ends without the distractions of politics. Although the political ramifications of these ideas are today considered "radical" when taken to their natural logical conclusions, the ideas themselves (such as the importance of respecting consent choices) are simple, intuitive, and broadly held. Clearly, political discussions on this topic are inevitable, but they are relegated to a section at the end to not distract from the main point: to describe the fundamental link between consent and morality.

This book project started after an internet conversation surrounding the question, "Is morality a subjective value or an objective, universal concept?" The assertion being made was that because each individual has a different idea of what is and is not moral behavior, morality *itself* is subject only to the beliefs of the individual. This conversation ended with a discussion of well-known historical atrocities. I asked,

> ***If*** **morality is a subjective value — if it is defined by each person's subjective view of the world — how can anyone argue that what rulers such as Mao Zedong, Joseph Stalin, Pol Pot, and Idi Amin did was immoral? Didn't *they* believe what they were doing was perfectly moral?**

But the question wasn't limited to evil dictators. In this conversation the claim was also made that not just individuals decide the morality of their actions, but the culture itself plays a part. My response was similar to the previous one:

_If_ morality is a subjective value — if it is defined by the culture of the era or local custom — how can anyone argue that chattel slavery, the slaughter of Native Americans, female circumcision, child marriage, the murder of gays, the subjugation of women, etc., are immoral? Didn't the people who committed _those_ atrocities also think _they_ were acting in a perfectly moral manner?

This idea of a subjective morality bothered me, even though it's very clear that different people believe vastly different things about what are and are not immoral acts. So I asked what may seem to be a ridiculous question:

What was it, specifically, that _made_ these acts immoral?

One possibility is that committing such actions is an overall detriment to humankind; that on the whole, these actions reduce the chances of the species surviving. We therefore evolved aversions to murder and atrocities as a fundamental requirement for existence.

But I don't see evolution entering into the larger connection we have with _morality_. If someone commits an atrocity, we don't denounce the action because it harms the species. Most people can see how bad actions would affect themselves and so intuitively don't want to inflict harm. Most people _do_ possess empathy for others. Even if we haven't experienced an atrocity ourselves, every one of us has experienced loss or seen loved ones be the victim of crimes. Those of us with young children can imagine the difficulty they would have in life if we, their parents, were not there. The intuition we feel about right and wrong actions can then be reduced to two points, based on empathy of others, and preservation of self:

> **People object to hurting or killing others because *they* can see the pain in others.**

> **People object to hurting or killing others because *they* do not want to be hurt or killed.**

But these points alone are not enough. There needs to be something that answers the question of *why a person's mere objection to an act* enters into that act being immoral at all. This is the very question the book in your hands attempts to explore.

It is with regret, however, that a number of very interesting topics must be set to the side in order to stay focused on that goal. Too many times the phrase "beyond the scope" (or its equivalent) is mentioned. Please understand that it is not my intention to side-step the discussion of any topic, only that whatever conclusions could be made from a side-point exploration doesn't get us closer to why consent and morality are connected.

Moreover, I freely admit that upon further reflection beyond this book, the reader may discover aspects of it that are unresolvable — aspects which may expose a contradiction even though I have taken great pains to avoid them. I do not take it as a failure of the arguments in this book if someone finds a bizarre situation that is not answered by correct application of the stated fundamental concepts. I take solace in the knowledge that no system can ever exist that is both consistent and complete.[2] So if you find an inconsistency or an idea that demonstrates incompleteness, congratulations; you've accomplished what I assumed someone could.

NOTE: I have used common names in many examples in the book. The names are chosen randomly, and have no connection with actual people.

---

2 Some will recognize this as stemming from Gödel's Incompleteness Theorem. (https://plato.stanford.edu/entries/goedel-incompleteness/) I assume any system I lay out is also subject to his theorem.

1.
Warm-Up

You don't have to make a judgment about the claim that's on the cover of this book quite yet. As a matter of fact, don't judge anything. You are safe here to take your mind out of defensive mode. This is a book. It can't do anything to harm you. All that is asked is for you to approach each idea and conclusion with some self-honesty. In other words, if you hear an idea or an explanation that makes sense, even if it goes against a long-held belief, it's okay to change your mind. You will never be asked to stop being yourself or give up your self-identity. You are only asked to have the willingness to honestly consider the ideas presented here.

Below are some questions to get going. Give these questions some time and consider each one a bit before moving on. You don't need to answer them now. Sometimes it's helpful to just let an idea simmer a bit in the mind.

1. Consider the situation where Ada violates the consent of Beth. Has Beth been wronged? *Why* has she been wronged?

2. If someone takes an action that only affects themselves, could it ever be said they did not consent to their own action?

3. Consider two random adults in the world who don't know each other. Can one of them give consent *for* the other?

4. Does the word "immoral" merely mean "unnatural," "disgusting," "indecent," "repugnant," "shameful," "scandalous," "loathsome," or otherwise "offensive to the sensibilities?"

5. If a person truly consented to an activity or an action that affects them, can they honestly believe that they are being immoral?

6. Can a person both consent *and* withhold consent to the same act at the same time?

7. Is it wrong to use the threat of violence against an otherwise peaceful person as motivation for them to act?

8. Should the morality of a particular action (if that action is right or wrong) be judged using the same method for anyone who does it, regardless of their job or intent?

2.
Definitions

The following terms are used in this book in the manner described below. Despite there being many different interpretations of these words, we must have a mutual understanding of how they are being used in this book in order to accomplish clear communication. This is not an assertion that these are the *only* definitions for the following words as they are used in society. You may even disagree with the definitions given here, but that should not detract from the underlying ideas. Terms that need a more detailed examination will be described in their own chapters.

Act/Action

An act (or an action) is the physical manifestation of *human intent*. For the purposes of this writing, an act or an action is taken by one single human, with the intent to alter their environment from a state which is less preferable for the actor to a state which is more preferable.

An act does not need to effectively result in what the actor intended. A carnival patron may pay money to throw a dart at a balloon, but he may miss his target. This is still an act. The patron had the intention to improve his environment (by obtaining a prize at low cost), and he undertook specific, purposeful action in an attempt to bring his intention into reality. The actual outcome of the action plays no part in determining if a person acted. Sometimes an action accomplishes the intent of the actor, sometimes it does not.

Accidental or unconscious movements are not actions. Accidentally leaving money on a park bench is not an act. *Intentionally* leaving money on a park bench (say, with the desire to film reactions of people for a documentary) is an act. Sleepwalking is another example of *not* acting because it carries no conscious human intent.

Merely thinking to one's self is not acting because it does not affect the world in any way outside the mind of the thinker. Certainly, self-reflection could improve the thinker's attitude toward their environment; they may be more willing to accept a less-than-preferable situation, but this is not acting toward making it a more preferable one. Thinking may lead to ideas which may *drive* actions, but internal thoughts themselves are not actions.

Coerced actions can also fall into the category of a human intending to improve his environment. A street thug who uses a gun to demand money from a victim is forcing the victim to make a choice from a few bad options: Give up the money? Run? Fight? Negotiate? None of them is ideal, but the victim will choose one in order to improve his current situation — namely, to separate himself from the criminal as quickly and cheaply as possible. Regardless of which option from this short list the victim chooses, he does in fact take an action in an attempt to improve his situation. The victim must weigh which risk he is willing to take to end the confrontation, but ultimately he takes *some* action. An example of a coerced action that does not fall into this category is if someone were to *physically overpower* and entirely control another person's body or a part of it.

Groups *do not* act. Each individual in a group acts. Common English usage often makes this confusing. A news story might report, "The city council acted to block the construction of a shopping mall." Readers may intuitively know what this means, but it is just a short-cut for saying, "The individual members of the city council voted, and the majority of votes declared a denial of permission for the owners of a construction company to orchestrate labor and capital to build a shopping mall. Should any of the owners of the construction company continue taking action to build, other individuals, at the direction of individual members of the council, could potentially take actions to physically stop anyone attempting to construct the mall."

This shortcut (of referring to groups as actors) applies to any group that is thought of as acting: a company, a government, an army, a protest march, a union, a gang, a charity, etc. When a group appears to act, it is forever and always some *specific* individual (or particular individuals) choosing to act on the group's behalf.

Lower brain functions — such as the ones that cause our heartbeats, our sneezes, or our jumps when we're startled — are not considered actions because they do not intend to improve a person's environment. Note that non-acts certainly can improve a person's environment. An involuntary sneeze could clear the sinuses making it easier to breathe, but without purposeful action, such an outcome would just be a pleasant happenstance.

Acting against

Every act has a human source and a receiver that could be human or non-human. When Alice stands from a sitting position, she "acts against" the Earth by pushing down with her legs, propelling herself up. Alice is the actor and the Earth is the receiver which was acted against. When a metalsmith creates a knife blade in her forge, she "acts against" the hot steel. The metalsmith is the human creating the action, and the steel is the receiver of the action. The term "acting against" isn't always negative. It merely means there is an actor (the person who acts) and a receiver of an act (an object, another person, or even the actor themselves).

No act can be taken that does not have a target. A person alone in the desert who makes the conscious decision to scream to no one is still doing so for a purpose. Perhaps it gives them an emotional release, or maybe they just want to see if there's an echo. If there were absolutely no reason to scream, the person would not scream. Someone who is delirious with heat, however, and screams unknowingly, is not acting.

Agency

Agency is a person's *ability* to act. More specifically, agency is the ability of an individual to *choose the acts* they take.

Agency is something that can be taken by or given away to other people. When you act, you are exercising your agency. When you choose to drink water instead of soda, when you choose to watch a movie instead of going on social media, you are exercising your agency. You are making an independent decision of your own will, free of restriction. No one can have infinite agency as we are all bound by physics. Few of us have agency to go to the Moon. But just as one hundred years ago, no one had agency to travel around the world in a matter of days, perhaps even space travel will be a common option for individuals to exercise their agency.

While our agency is sometimes limited by nature, it can also be limited by other people or even by our own choices. A person who hires a chauffeur voluntarily gives up a tiny bit of agency. For the time they are being driven, they do not have the direct ability to control where they are being taken. When a person orders dinner in a restaurant, they lose the ability to directly control the ingredients in their food and therefore lose a bit of agency. If a police officer handcuffs you and places you in his car under threat of violence, he has taken away nearly all of your agency.[3]

---

3 You still keep the option to speak or not speak.

Aggression

An aggression is the initiation of an action against an innocent or peaceful person which aims to violate that person's consent via physical harm of them or their property. Aggressions also include the use of overt, credible, and specific *threats* of physical violence in an attempt to coerce another person into taking a desired action (or inaction). The word "aggression" is most commonly used here as a noun. As in, "Adam has committed an aggression against Bill."

The act of committing an aggression is *always* a violation of consent, but not all violations of consent are aggressions, as some violations can be accidental or harmless. An action that does not violate a person's consent cannot be an aggression. Even negligence does not always rise to the level of aggression.

Authority

In this book, the word "authority" means to have *control over someone or something*. "Authority" is used here as a noun, but throughout the book the word is almost always qualified (as in, "legitimate authority" or "limited authority").

A person can be *granted* authority, or a person can *assert* authority, but in all cases, whether peacefully or forcefully gained, "authority" is used to describe a very *specific* authority (control) over a piece of property or a person. It is *not* used in reference to an expert such as, "Professor Smith is an authority on the subject" or as an elected or government actor as in, "The authorities prosecuted the offender."

Legitimate

An act or a state of being that is in accordance with first (or, *a priori*) principles is considered to be legitimate. These principles will be covered in depth later, but for the purposes of this definition the principles are "peaceful, voluntary, and consensual." The term "legitimate" should not be confused with the idea of being "legal." When something is "legalized," it has been artificially "legitimized" by those who do not have the authority to grant such legitimacy. For example, chattel slavery of humans was never a legitimate property claim regardless of its codification into "law" or being "legitimized" by governments.

Conversely, an action or state of being that is illegitimate is accomplished in an *improper* manner by way of *violating* first principles or any other principles derived from them. Most often, this word is used with "authority" as in "legitimate authority" which means having control over a person or property which was gained via the first principles of peace and mutually consensual choices.

Ownership

When a person has the legitimate authority to control a physical thing, it can be said the person owns it. Under the umbrella of ownership, there are several separate aspects of control an individual can exert over a piece of property. Namely, an owner can:

- Possess (hold in a constant state without action)

- Use (consume to gain utility)

- Transfer (give or sell permanently)

- Lend (transfer for a temporary period)

- Destroy (permanently eliminate all remaining utility)

- Exclude (prevent others from any of the above)

The reason these actions of ownership are broken out into separate aspects is because each one can be transferred in whole, or even in part, to others. These transfers can be made with or without separate agreements for compensation. For example, if Mia owns a home, she can lend it to others by temporarily transferring to them her legitimate authority to use it. The new users of the home have now obtained their own limited authority to exclude others, such as a burglar, which is a power granted to them by Mia, the owner. (This limited authority to exclude others may even include Mia herself under certain circumstances.) In turn, they may have the additional authority to lend part of the home to others (say, to rent an empty room) depending on the original use agreement.

Not all lending includes a use authority. The owner of a rare piece of art may lend it to a museum for a limited time. By loaning it, the owner of the artwork temporarily transfers only the authority to possess it and a limited authority to exclude others.

Owners can make contracts to transfer some of these authorities based on certain conditions. The act of receiving money, with the condition of granting the lender of the money ownership in the condition of non-repayment, is the essence of collateralization.

Owners can even make agreements to simply voluntarily not exercise a particular power. An owner who purchases insurance agrees that if he intentionally destroys his property, he will not receive compensation for its loss.

Peaceful person

A "peaceful person" is a person who has not violated the consent of others. In other words, it is someone who has not committed an aggression against others. However, in most instances a reference to, for example, "a peaceful person, Carol," means Carol has not committed an aggression against Dylan. This distinction is important because Carol certainly *may have* committed aggressions against Ellen and Frank, but there are times when it helps to make a point when only considering the direct relationship between two individual people. An example is if Carol is quietly sitting on her front steps and Dylan walks by, Carol is considered to be a "peaceful person" if she does not violate Dylan's consent and has not violated Dylan's consent in the past.

3.
First Principles

This list of first principles does not even scratch the surface in terms of completely explaining the fullness of each idea. There is simply not enough space here to do them proper justice, but at least some understanding of these principles is necessary to achieve the final goal of establishing a link between consent and morality. There are countless volumes written on each topic, and the reader is highly encouraged to explore them, some of which are cited at the end of this book.

Cogito, ergo sum; Je pense, donc je suis; I think, therefore I am

It may seem silly to start at the very beginning, but it is vital to establish that humans, in fact, exist. It would be trivially easy to dismiss the entire topic of consent and morality if humanity itself is nonexistent.

The point of René Descartes' famous saying,[4] for the purposes of establishing a framework for consent and morality, was better phrased by Antoine Léonard Thomas as "*dubito, ergo cogito, ergo sum*" translated in English as, "I doubt, therefore I think, therefore I am."[5] Doubting your existence is a unique, independent act which itself demonstrates that you do, in fact, exist. Conversely, if you did not exist, you would not be here to doubt your existence.[6]

Asserting your non-existence as an existing being is committing what is called a *performative contradiction* — your very attempt to assert something disproves your assertion. It would be as if someone said the words, "I do not know how to say a sentence in English." The assertion is self-disproving because saying a sentence in English is conclusive proof you know how to say a sentence in English.[7]

The requirement to avoid contradictions is an important part of establishing later principles. It is a critical logical building block that is so important it has its own principle — the principle of non-contradiction.

---

4 https://la.wikisource.org/wiki/Principia_philosophiae#Non_posse_a_nobis

5 http://www.gutenberg.org/files/13846/13846-h/13846-h.htm

6 Even if you only existed as a program in a giant alien super-computer, you would still exist in some form in order to consider your existence.

7 This is true even if you don't understand what you're actually saying. See: https://www.youtube.com/watch?v=6vgoEhsJORU

Principle of non-contradiction

The principle of non-contradiction (PNC) is the intuitive concept that says something cannot be both 'X' and 'not-X' at the same time.[8] A person cannot both take an action and not take that action simultaneously. A ball thrown into the air cannot be both rising and not-rising with respect to the ground. (It can be neither rising nor falling, but it cannot be *both* rising *and* either stationary or falling.) This point has already been touched on with performative contradictions: no assertion which disproves itself can be true. The PNC is a more general understanding of contradictions: *Any* idea, statement, assertion, or belief that results in a contradiction cannot be correct.

Self-ownership

Each human being holds an immutable ownership claim on themselves — their body, their actions, their time, and their life.

The proof of this is shown by use of performative contradiction: If Ethan were to argue that he does not own himself, Ethan must consciously employ thoughts and movements (fingers typing or words spoken) to make that argument. These thoughts and movements require him to have ownership control over these faculties. Again, the act of making the assertion (denial of

---

8 https://plato.stanford.edu/entries/aristotle-noncontradiction

self-ownership) proves the assertion false. (Acts that demonstrate ownership authority must be employed in the denial itself.)

This ownership claim includes all the acts previously mentioned under the umbrella of ownership with one single exception: Human beings cannot permanently transfer ownership of themselves to others. There is a counterargument to self-ownership that suggests that if we truly owned ourselves, we could "sell ourselves into permanent slavery."

Set aside the fact that such an option itself doesn't *disprove* the fact that humans own themselves. (It would actually go a long way to prove it.) There is a problem with this line of reasoning: attempting to do so — to sell one's self into irreversible slavery — creates a contradiction.

Assume for a moment that a human (a self-owner) *could* sell themselves into permanent slavery to another person, thus no longer having an ownership claim on themselves. The new owner would need the capacity to fully control the agency of their purchase. Full control of another person's agency must include all of their ability to act independently. Anything less would not be ownership, as the seller would still be retaining some amount of agency: the very property that was assumed to be fully transferred. In order to totally prevent any of the seller's thoughts from creating independent action (and therefore exercising his agency), the buyer would need to control every tiny movement of the seller at all times. This would be functionally equivalent to controlling an inanimate body, which by definition is not slavery but the destruction of an entire human being in the creation of an automaton. The seller would also be required to permanently assign *any possible future ability* to act independently to the new owner. So long as the seller has an independent human mind, this is a physical impossibility.

Because a complete transfer of one's ownership in themselves to another is impossible, it *is a contradiction* because the original premise was that a human *could* sell his entire ownership stake in himself. If denying self-ownership creates a contradiction and taking one of the actions of ownership against ourselves (permanent transfer) *also* creates a contradiction, we must conclude that this single action normally available in the ownership of other property simply does not exist in human self-ownership. This is not to say that such an act is "denied" by anyone or that any of the others are contradictory. It is only to say that such an act is impossible and therefore is merely *absent* in the set of ownership actions available to self-owners.

There is another, much more relevant issue to the denial of self-ownership in terms of the topic of this book: without self-ownership, *there is no authority* to withhold consent. Much more will be covered on that topic in the section on consent.

Equivalence principle

In order to understand the claim that consent is equivalent to morality, it is critical to understand the idea of equivalency.

If there are two (or more) apparently different things which are truly indistinguishable from one another, it can be said they are equivalent. If someone says they have one dozen eggs, or if they say they have twelve eggs, those two methods of referring to the same eggs are indistinguishable. These alternative methods of referring to a quantity of twelve are therefore equivalent.

A more complex example, but one much better suited for explaining the equivalence between morality and consent, is Albert Einstein's equivalence principle.[9] A more complete description of it can be found online, but in order to properly tie it to the topic, it is explained in brief here.

Imagine for a moment you are in an entirely enclosed room. There are no windows, and no sounds or vibrations can enter, so it is silent except for any noises you make in the room itself. There is light in the room so you can see the tables, chairs, or whatever objects populate it. (And for those who like to be particular about such things, there is a method to generate fresh oxygen so you can breathe.) In this room, you can sit on the floor or in a chair. You can climb up onto a table and jump off. When you lift things, they are heavy. By all appearances, you are simply standing, sitting, jumping, and living in a normal room. We will call you the "internal observer" because you are only observing the environment *inside* the room.

No information about the outside world can get to you. Therefore, as the internal observer, you have absolutely no ability whatsoever to know if you are in a room resting on the surface of the Earth or if you are in a room accelerating through space at the *same rate* of Earth's gravitational force.

---

9 https://www.einstein-online.info/en/spotlight/equivalence_principle/

In every literal sense, if you were in space in a rocket accelerating with the same force as Earth's gravity, unless there were external indications (such as a window, or the sound of an engine, etc.) you would feel as if you were sitting quietly on *terra firma*.

Conversely, if all the objects — including yourself — suddenly begin floating and bouncing around the room, you would not have any way of knowing if you were in a space ship that had stopped accelerating or if you were, say, in a suspended room (such as an elevator) that was dropped from a distance above the ground (until it crashed, of course).

It is because of this inability to tell the difference between being stationary in a gravitational field on the ground or being accelerated through space that gravity and acceleration are considered *equivalent*.

If it is impossible to tell the difference between two things, they are equivalent.

Notice, however, that an "external observer" — one who is outside the sealed room — can clearly tell if you were grounded or accelerating through space. Understanding this difference between an observer inside the room and an observer outside the room is absolutely critical to understanding the larger concept of equivalence between consent and morality. The following is one of the most important points in this book:

Even though one person observing *inside* the room sees and experiences an entirely different view

than someone else observing *outside* the room, this in *no way diminishes the fact that gravity and acceleration are equivalent.*

Gravity and acceleration are equivalent because of the very fact that the person inside the room cannot distinguish between them. Someone outside of the room making their own observation does not negate the *real and objective* observations being made inside the room. The only reason the outside observer "knows" what is happening to the room is because they are comparing the room to *their own* observations of the world *other than* the room itself.

But does the outside observer *really* know what the "truth" is? After all, what if the outside observer was also within a larger enclosed room? Would *they* be able to know if they *and the room they were observing* were all together sitting on Earth or accelerating through space? No, the outside observer would not. The same rule applies to *all* observers:

To all people in all places at all times, when two things are indistinguishable, they are equivalent.

Once consent and morality are explored later, it will be shown how moral and immoral acts are indistinguishable from consensual and non-consensual acts, respectively.

4.
Consent

Consent is a simple idea. The essential concept — to give permission — is very straightforward. Its meaning in practice is highly intuitive. "Do you consent to this procedure?" "You need to sign this consent form." "I don't consent to being searched." With close examination, however, it becomes clear just how complex the idea of consent really is.

Consent defined

For the purposes of this book, a more descriptive definition of consent is necessary:

> **Consent is explicitly affirmed and voluntary acceptance of an action affecting one's self or one's own honestly acquired property.**

Within this more precise definition there are a number of ideas that need additional explanation.

"Explicitly affirmed"

The range of methods by which people explicitly affirm (i.e., clearly communicate) consent is vast and highly dependent on the environment and situation. In a store, consent for a trade is expressed by placing a product on the cashier's counter and then actually paying for the product. For exchanging a piece of land, a written agreement with witnessed signatures is the norm in American society. In an auction, the consent to purchase an expensive piece of art could be made with the raising of a single finger.

The purpose of explicit affirmation is to prevent misunderstanding. Someone interested in getting a tattoo may choose a design, sit down with the artist, and agree to the placement of the stencil. However, none of this *truly* affirms the consent to have their skin marked for the rest of their life. There may be second thoughts. One last "Ready to do this?" can go a long way to ensure that consent has been given.

"Voluntary acceptance"

When a person makes a decision (such as whether or not to consent to an act), that decision is either voluntary or involuntary.

An *involuntary* decision is a decision made under duress or coercion where the coercion was intentionally brought on by another person. A decision made without duress or coercion is always considered voluntary.

Of course, there are many potential decisions that involve some level of duress that are still considered voluntary. The key is to identify the *source* of the duress. Nature can be very forceful, but nature does not have agency. One cannot withhold consent from nature. If Zachery is under duress to make a decision, and the duress he is under was not brought by a person (or if it wasn't brought intentionally), then whatever decision Zachery makes is still considered to be voluntary.

For example, you run a delivery business and depend heavily on your van being in working order. While making a delivery one day, you hit a tree that fell in the road making your van undrivable until it's repaired. You get estimates from a few body shops and decide to bring your van to Fast Repair Body Shop.[10]

Would anyone reasonably suggest that the owner of Fast Repair Body Shop put you under duress to spend your money at his business? Did the *tree* put you under duress? This is a case of a naturally occurring event, and nature is not a person. Nature is not a thinking, rational entity and therefore cannot *intend* to do anything.

Consider a scenario where you have zero chance of getting a ticket for running a red light at a busy intersection. Would you do it? For rational people, they would probably not run the red. Why not? The most obvious answer is you know the other direction of traffic has the green light, and by entering the intersection when you see a red light, it vastly increases your chance of causing a serious crash.

---

10 This name is fictitious.

Did the other drivers *coerce* you into not running the red light? Even though this is a completely human-made situation (not a natural one), we intuitively know that no one is *intentionally* introducing duress or coercion. Without a particular person applying intentional coercion (such as a police officer ready to give you a ticket), your choice in that moment to *not* run the red light was a voluntary one.

Now say you pull up to a red light at a desolate intersection. You can see for five miles in all directions and there isn't a vehicle in sight... other than the police officer looking at you just off the road. Do you run the red light?

If it took you six seconds to cross the intersection, a vehicle that's five miles away would need to be going 3,000 miles per hour in order to hit you before you made it across. It is quite obvious to you there is zero chance of you causing a crash by running the red light.

However, rational people would not run the red for the simple reason that they know what getting a ticket means: loss of property (in fines), loss of time, perhaps increased insurance rates, etc. In this situation, you are being coerced by a specific individual to not safely cross the intersection until the automatic light changes to green. Your choice to remain motionless at the intersection was *not* voluntary.

"Actions affecting one's self"

With some exceptions that will be covered later in this chapter, someone else cannot give your consent to an action that affects you. You cannot give someone else's consent to an action that affects them. Ellen cannot consent for Frank. Consent is deciding *for yourself* what others can and cannot do *to you* or your property.

"One's own honestly-acquired property"

As mentioned, property that is acquired "honestly" — that is, through mutually voluntary methods, and not using force, coercion, intentional fraud, etc. — is *legitimately* owned. If you used previously-acquired resources (so long as those resources were also gained honestly) to obtain a thing, that thing is as much a part of "you" as the time you spent (which is legitimately yours) to obtain it.

For example, you find a way to arrange small rocks and items from nature into forms of art. You spend your days looking for raw materials while ensuring that what you collect are not already someone else's property, you bring them home, and arrange them into art. You then attend art fairs to trade them for a price you believe is fair. People offer you money for your art. You accept the money in trade voluntarily, and the person giving you the money also does so voluntarily. In this example, the entire process of gathering materials, creating art, then selling it is ultimately just you exchanging your legitimately owned resource — your time — for money.

The money you hold after selling your art belongs to you. It belongs to you in the exact same way the *art* belonged to you earlier in the day. The art belonged to you as much as the *time* you spent making your art belonged to you. If someone steals your artwork, they steal from you the time and energy needed to create it. If someone steals your money, they have stolen all the time you took to create the art *and* the time and energy needed to display and sell your creations to patrons of the art fairs.

Instead of simply taking your artwork, imagine if the thief had threatened you with physical violence to go find rocks, assemble them into art, then hand him the finished piece to keep. The direct theft of a person's time used for the benefit of others has a name: slavery.

> **The act of stealing someone's property, including money (which is simply a different form of property), is *equivalent* to the act of enslaving the person for the time needed to produce it.**

From where does the ability to consent originate?

Simply put, your authority to give or withhold consent originates from your self-ownership and your agency. Your agency originates from your humanity. Specifically, agency originates from your cognitive and physical power to make choices. Your self-ownership is the source of your authority to make consent decisions regarding yourself and any property you have legitimately acquired.

Informed consent

In an ideal world, all consent would be perfectly informed. Being "fully-informed" is a condition where a person entering into an agreement or consenting to an act knows all the risks, all the options, all the ramifications, and all the alternatives to what they're agreeing to. Unfortunately, such a condition does not exist. Obtaining perfect information is physically impossible because there is no limit to the number of alternatives, and many risks are unknowable by anyone.

A person does not need to possess perfect information in order to be considered "informed." At a minimum, the idea of being "informed" means being free from *intentional misinformation*. Ultimately, each person is responsible for their own knowledge. There can be no reasonable requirement to force others to inform you of every possible fact regarding a transaction or necessarily even "important" facts. What is important varies widely from person to person and even from agreement to agreement between the same people. If Julie wishes to buy a hybrid car, and gas mileage is her primary concern, she may see the value on the new car sticker. But that number was determined under a small range of conditions the manufacturer considered "reasonable."

Julie knows she must drive through steep canyons every day to and from work. The manufacturer could not have accounted for her specific need nor could it be expected to inform Julie of the precise mileage she will get in her *exact* situation. If Julie decides to buy the car, she is giving her informed consent to make the trade. Of course, she would be more informed if she reached out to other owners of the same model car who drive under similar conditions in order to gain from their experience. Doing this kind of research is entirely *her* responsibility. Unless the manufacturer gave intentional falsehoods about the car's performance or terms of the trade, the buyer is assumed to be informed. Any alternative world where an expectation is placed on one party to "fully inform" the other falls into the trap where there is no articulable limit of what is expected. Forever and always there will be something more they "should have" disclosed.

It can certainly be argued that even in a situation where no fraud or misrepresentation took place, there may be imbalances of knowledge that can be exploited.

For example, the seller of a house personally knows a city council member who told them an airport is in the planning stages, and their house will be on the border under the landing zone. This example suggests there are *ethical* reasons to inform the other party beyond mere abstinence of fraud. The more permanent the act or trade will be for one side, the greater the ethical standards should be.

The medical field is a common example where ethics demand giving patients information regarding risks and alternatives beyond what is normally expected from an everyday transaction. But even in this situation, there is a limit. Should a doctor list each and every complication the patient could conceivably have with every procedure? Overburdening a patient with minutiae that probably won't apply to them is also a disservice.

One example of where one side of an exchange has intentionally tilted every trade in their favor is a casino. Casinos only offer games that have a "house edge." This means the casino is either more likely to win, or if they lose, the player is paid less than what is justified by the chances of winning the game originally.

Even having *every transaction* artificially imbalanced in their favor, a casino is not required to explain exactly how much of an edge they have, the likelihood of a player winning, or if there is any optimum strategy of play to reduce the casino's edge. The player is expected to know this. The existence of countless websites and publications dedicated to helping players understand these aspects are evidence that the burden of knowledge is in fact on the player and that the players themselves know the burden is on them.

While this idea of *caveat emptor*[11] can be taken to an extreme, it's not always easy to determine where informed consent ends and fraud begins. Continuing with the gambling example, "Three-card Monty" is a common street game where sleight-of-hand and collusion are used to deceive players betting on the final location of one of three cards. The dealer did not explicitly *say* he was not going to use sleight of hand. Was the player defrauded out of their money, or could it be said the player was merely paying for some entertainment? How does this compare to carnival games which are either nearly impossible to win or only winnable by people of extreme physical skill such as professional athletes? Is there an expectation by the carnival to explain why each game is so difficult?

---

11 Let the buyer beware.

As a patron or buyer, your trading partner cannot be expected to completely inform you of every possible fact about a trade. There will always be some aspect of the trade unknown to even the most well-meaning person. Consider the reverse: Should the seller of an item expect the buyer to inform her of the inflationary (dropping in value) nature of the money she's accepting? Isn't that a fact many sellers would find important? Any attempt to place such a burden on one side of a trade or the other is purely arbitrary. It's helpful to remember that in reality, there is no 'buying' or 'selling' but only trading between two individual human beings who deserve only that the trade is not coerced or made under intentionally false pretenses.

Has consent been given?

The question of whether or not consent has been given is certainly an important one. It probably won't take the astute reader long to come up with many real-world situations when consent signals are ambiguous.

Although determining *when* someone has consented can be challenging, examining the link between consent and morality doesn't require an objective method of determining if someone has actually made their consent choice clear to others. For our purposes here, we can assume a person making a consent choice has either demonstrated their explicit affirmation in a way acceptable given the circumstances or withheld their consent by making their denial clear (or by not giving an indication either way[12]).

---

12 Either consent has been given or it has not. There is no middle ground. Not giving an

Of course, there can be great disagreement between people if someone gave ambiguous signals regarding their consent, which is why high-value agreements between strangers involve very clear signs of consent. Buying a house, buying a car, entering a contract, business-to-business agreements, etc., are rarely, if ever, completed on a spoken word. These agreements are carefully crafted, and signs of consent are demonstrable and unambiguous.

No one can know how the affirmation of consent will be accomplished in the future. Electronic signatures are beginning to replace physical signatures. Blockchain technology could create a system by which some consent choices are publicly viewable and part of a permanent record. Exactly *how* it is determined that consent has been given may change through time, but *respecting* consent choices does not change because consent is inexorably connected to the human condition.

Regardless of what methods people have traditionally used to determine if consent has been given, and regardless of what methods will be used in the future, the process of determining if consent is given is entirely independent of the connection between morality and consent.

Withholding consent

At any time, for any reason, or for no reason at all, human beings can withhold their consent from any action taken against them. This is true

indication is the same as explicitly refusing to give consent.

Methods by which consent is determined

Consent is equivalent to morality

A handy Venn diagram showing where the set of methods by which consent choices are demonstrated connect with consent being equivalent to morality.

even if they had previously consented.[13] People can *withhold* consent for the same reason they can *grant* consent — because of the ownership we hold in ourselves. *Only owners* have the legitimate authority to exclude others from acting against what they own (either themselves or their property). If you don't own something, you have no position to stop the legitimate owner from using it, lending it, or taking any of the other actions an owner can take against their property.

The owner of an apple can exclude others from eating it. The owner of a car can exclude others from driving it. The owner of a home can exclude others from entry. Conversely, the apple's owner can consent to others eating some

---

13 There are some specific exceptions to this that will be explored in a later section.

or all of it. The car's owner can lend it to their friend, and a home's owner can rent it to others.

People often consent to an action under certain conditions but then withhold consent if conditions change. For example, you may consent to purchase a television if the price is $600 but not if the price is $800. You may consent to lend your friend your car, but if your child needs to see the doctor, you may decide to withhold your consent because you have a new, urgent need to use it. Boxers consent to be physically hit when they enter the ring, but at any moment they can end the fight, declare their intent to stop fighting, and withhold their consent to continue being hit; any intentional hitting that occurs after the fight has ended would be no different (in terms of violating consent) from one boxer hitting the other without consent while walking down the street.

Similarly, you are the only one with legitimate authority to exclude others from using you. This includes the parts of you that were mentioned earlier: your time, your body, your life. No other human being has the legitimate authority to force you to work for their benefit without your consent. That would be theft of your time and use of your body — commonly called slavery. No other human being has the legitimate authority to harm you or kidnap you. And although it should go without saying, no one has the legitimate authority to murder another human being.

It should be made clear, however, that even though any person can at any moment withhold consent they have previously given, that does not mean there will be no consequences for doing so.

For example, the buyer of a new car takes out a loan against it under the agreement that if he fails to make timely payments, the car will be repossessed. Under such an agreement, the ownership claim over the car remains with the lender, *not* the borrower/driver. The borrower is of course a self-owner, and his money is his own property. Therefore, he is completely free to withhold his consent to making payments. The inevitable consequence of withholding consent to make payments is the lender will take their car back. In this example, the act of repossession isn't theft; it's simply the legitimate property owner taking physical possession of their property under the terms of a contract freely and voluntarily entered into by the borrower.

Another example is the boxer who, by withholding his consent to keep fighting, has likely lost the match and may not be booked to fight in larger, higher-paying matches. The consequences don't always need to be severe or violent, however. If you are regularly consenting to lend your friend your car and just as regularly revoking that consent, eventually your friend will no longer trust you. A movie actor who has a habit of pulling out of productions will find it more difficult to be hired than one who keeps their commitments.

Implied consent

It is often argued that certain behaviors or circumstances can demonstrate consent without an individual needing to explicitly affirm it. When consent is assumed to have been given based on factors other than direct affirmation, this is called "implied consent." For example, you cannot withhold consent based on your physical location. That your mere presence within a predetermined area, be it a country, a private home, or anything in between, constitutes an implied (i.e., assumed) consent to certain actions taken against you.

This is false. Implied consent is simply one person making an assumption that another person has consented regardless of explicit affirmation. If a woman wears a revealing dress, it cannot be implied merely from her choice of clothing that she has consented to be touched inappropriately.

Consent cannot be assumed. It must *always* be explicit. Self-ownership does not vanish when a human being wears certain clothes or crosses an arbitrary line in the dirt. It *is* possible that a person may temporarily give up a bit of agency; e.g., someone who rents a room may not play loud music if the homeowner forbids it. But voluntarily consenting to give up agency is very different from implying consent.

Why is consenting to give up agency not the same as implied consent? Isn't the homeowner just using her ownership authority to override the renter's self-ownership authority? No, because the renter does not possess the legitimate authority to enter the home in first place. It *seems* to be a conflict, but it's notable that there was an earlier consent given by the homeowner under a specific condition: "I consent to you renting a room in my home so long as you do not play loud music" — to which the renter *also* consented. When both parties (such as a homeowner and a tenant) consent to the same agreement, it is a mutual consent. Mutual consent can never be a situation that involves force.[14]

Even if no such condition was given, the owner of a property can always revoke consent at any time:[15] "I'm sorry, I know I didn't tell you not to play loud music, but my baby can't sleep when you play it." The renter's consent to this is not implied. The renter can play his music as loud as he wishes — anywhere else but within the homeowner's property.

If you enter a restaurant and order a meal, there *appears* to be an implicit consent to pay for it. As mentioned, explicit consent can be expressed differently in different situations. In this example, consent is *explicitly given* during the act of ordering the meal because you made a clear request for a product and services.

It's not very difficult to find examples that demonstrate the dangers of implying consent. Imagine a person saying the following:

"You can't revoke consent. You *live* here. Living here is *implied* consent."

Can you tell who is making this claim? Is it a citizen explaining why someone must pay his taxes, or is it a husband making nightly demands of his wife?

---

14 If one side uses force, it is no longer mutual consent.

15 Those knowledgeable of tricky property ownership issues may recall the famous "hot air balloon" problem. Due to the level of detail needed to explore this classic problem, it will be examined in the moral dilemma section.

Consenting for others

Consent originates entirely from within the person who has the authority to grant it — and from no one else.

Other than narrow and specific exceptions outlined in the next section, throughout the regular course of a person's life, no one else can consent for them or withhold consent for them (without their consent, of course).

In other words, unless you and I have some prearranged agreement (such as power of attorney), I cannot consent for you, and you cannot consent for me. This is because you own you, and I own me. I can't give your consent because I don't own you, and you can't give my consent because you don't own me. This is similar to the idea that you cannot lend my car to your friend because you don't own my car, and I cannot sell your works of art because I don't own your art.

The *social implications* of people being able to consent for others are enormous. If Jack can somehow obtain the legitimate authority to consent for you, he can consent for some or all your property to be transferred to him. He can consent for you to hire him for his services at any price he wishes. Jack could consent for you to take whatever medicines he decides. He could even consent for you to give up your parental authority in your children. In other words, no society that wishes to survive can suffer a culture that accepts the ability for some people to obtain such authority over others without clear, informed, and expressed consent of the specific individual who is giving up that authority.

The exact same principle holds for withholding consent as it does with giving consent. You cannot withhold my consent, and I cannot withhold your consent. If a car owner consents to giving rides to strangers in exchange for money, no one has the authority to "withhold" the car owner's consent. In other words, no one can *deny them the ability* to consent. If a homeowner decides to rent their home to visitors, no one has the authority to withhold the homeowner's consent. Non-owners of property have no legitimate authority over that property. It doesn't belong to them. So as long as a property owner is not intentionally or negligently harming others, there is no mechanism by which a non-owner can obtain a legitimate authority over that property without the consent of the owner themselves.[16]

Not only do *I* not have the authority to consent for you, my friend cannot consent for you. My neighbor also cannot consent for you. So even if my

---

16 A brief digression here is in order because there is a common objection to this: "But if my neighbor rents their house to strangers, that act harms me because my property value will drop." To be blunt, no one "owns" the value of their home. The "value" of a home is merely a number that represents a history of the amount similar homes in the area have been selling for. If you sell your home, you will then own the proceeds of the sale. But a list of recently sold properties by no means creates an ownership claim in anything. A similar but even less compelling objection is, "I own a hotel, and homeowners renting below my costs cut into my income, which is harming me." No one owns potential income from unknown future customers. No one can claim that reducing future earnings (which may or may not even exist) is "harm." That would be like a book manufacturer claiming an e-book reader maker "harmed" them because people are buying fewer physical books. If people prefer paying for one thing over another and do so voluntarily, that's a consumer preference change, and no one "owns" consumer preferences other than the consumers themselves.

friend, my neighbor, and I get together, since none of us can individually consent for you, as a group we cannot consent for you either. We don't gain an ownership authority in you or your property just because three of us have decided we do. No person on my block can consent for you. No person in my city can consent for you.

In fact, *no human being in existence* — other than you[17] — has a natural, legitimate authority to grant or withhold your consent. Furthermore, no human being in existence can *obtain* a legitimate authority to grant or withhold your consent without your explicit consent.

Because no single individual has the authority to grant or withhold your consent, *and* no individual can gain that authority, then no *group* of individuals has the authority to grant or withhold your consent. Groups of people are not separate and distinct entities with agency; only individual people are capable of action (exercising their agency).

Even if a large group of people are all in agreement, that doesn't give them any authority over your consent choices. Every individual in a large group of people may *believe* they have an authority, but believing it does not grant them an authority you never explicitly affirmed. Because the *only* source of authority over your consent decisions is you, no matter how many people in a group say otherwise, the powerful conclusion we must reach is:

---

17 "You" being a conscious, able-minded adult. Some specific, limited exceptions are explored in a later section.

No *group of people*, merely by virtue of its size, has the legitimate authority to grant or withhold your consent.

Furthermore, *there is no mechanism* by which any other person can gain such authority other than through your explicitly affirmed and voluntary acceptance of it.

Violating consent

The act of violating a person's consent is the act of taking away their agency. It prevents them from exercising their ownership authority in whatever was the target of the violation: their property or themselves. The word "violation" comes directly from the Latin *violationem* meaning an injury, irreverence, desecration, or crime.[18]

There are countless ways in which one person can violate the consent of another person, and there are many levels of violation, from harmless, innocent accidents to intentional, violent acts. In all cases, the *intent* of the violator plays heavily in how the violation is viewed. Also, because all consent violations represent some kind of loss, the person whose consent was violated is due appropriate compensation from the violator, which could be anything between a simple apology to millions of dollars depending on the act and intent behind it. It should be noted that this is not a book on criminality or what the proper corrective actions should be

---

18 https://www.etymonline.com/word/violation

for different severities of consent violations. This section will not attempt to find resolutions for them. Doing so would not speak to the larger point that intent is the primary consideration when determining if a particular consent violation is a crime.

Crimes

Self-ownership, agency, consent, and morality are what create the concept of a crime in the first place. If you have no authority to withhold consent from actions, then other people could do what they wanted to you or your property, and there would be no legitimate option to object to their actions. There would be no recourse, and you would have no standing to be "made whole" because you wouldn't have actually lost anything. Interestingly, this is the exact reason why speech cannot be a crime: No one can withhold consent for others uttering or writing words[19] as doing so would create a contradiction. (A more detailed explanation will come later in the Exceptions section.)

Animals cannot commit crimes. Very young children cannot commit crimes. A person in the back seat of a taxi cannot commit the crime of

---

19 A person who commits libel or slander against you doesn't actually violate your consent because they do not directly harm anything to which you hold an ownership claim. Libel and slander (dishonestly) changes the view other people have of you. Your reputation is just that — the perception of you in the minds of other people. Since you do not have an ownership authority over other people's thoughts and beliefs, you have no authority to withhold consent from anyone wishing to change them.

"hit-and-run." The reason is, in all of these cases, there is no agency; none of these "actors" (neither the animal nor the child nor the passenger) have any ability to control the situation with purposeful intent. Therefore, they cannot be considered to be actors at all.

When one person *intentionally* violates another's consent regarding their person or their property, it can often be considered a crime. Keep in mind, the fact that a person has committed a crime doesn't automatically negate their innate ownership in themselves, causing them to lose all ability to withhold consent. A criminal, however, has *no authority to withhold consent* regarding the need to compensate their victims or receive punishment.[20] If they did have authority to withhold consent, the act of retrieving stolen property from them, for example, would simply be the commission of a new crime (as a violation of the criminal's own consent).

Imagine the situation where a thief steals your car and hides it on his property in a locked garage. Under normal circumstances, so long as he acquired the garage using peaceful and legitimate methods, no one else would have the authority to step onto the thief's property and enter his garage without his consent. (The thief is also a self-owning human being,

---

20 In this section it is assumed when a person is said to have committed a crime, they did in fact commit it. Clearly, a significant effort must be made to ensure those accused of committing crimes are actually guilty of committing them. In truth, there may never be any complete guarantee of accuracy regarding guilt and innocence. But these questions are not related to the core topic here — the implications of intentionally violating someone's consent.

his criminal actions notwithstanding.) But in this case, *your* property is physically in *his* garage. Clearly, the thief would not voluntarily consent to you trespassing and breaking into his garage. Since the car is your legitimate property, he has no authority to withhold consent if you[21] choose to retrieve it. Therefore, the minimum required actions you need to take to retrieve your property are not a violation of his consent. If you must trespass and physically break into his garage to retrieve your car, you are doing so only because of his act of theft — an aggression initiated against you and your property. Any additional actions (say, breaking an entire door down when a lock could be cut off or taking other things in his garage) would, in fact, be an additional crime.[22]

As mentioned, in a human society where there are concepts such as consent, morality, and crime, there are two acts from which a criminal has no authority to withhold consent:

1. Making the victim whole

2. Punishment

With property crimes (such as theft, destruction, and fraud), making the victim whole consists of:

---

21 "You" in this case is either yourself or someone you designate to act on your behalf.

22 A thief is by no means a sympathetic character, and few people feel a thief deserves mercy. The goal here is not leniency but accuracy. Criminals deserve to receive no less than the punishment for their violations of consent — but also no more.

A. Fully replacing property (or its value) stolen or gained through fraud

B. Compensation for loss of use

But the harm caused by the violation of consent regarding one's person is significantly more difficult to measure. The ideal goal of "being made whole" may not be possible. Crimes such as battery, kidnapping, rape, or murder, so long as human beings are finite creatures, will never truly have an objective measure of the damage caused by these acts in order to be "compensated." These highly complex questions are far beyond the scope of this book.[23]

As an aside, there are conceivable situations where it seems the ownership authority of two innocent people prevent each other from using their property. A more detailed examination of this possibility expands on the above example in the section on moral dilemmas.

Negligence

There are times when a person violates another's consent without the overt intention of doing so, yet they should have known their action (or inaction) was going to harm another person. Some examples include a truck

---

23 The likely best but by no means perfect solution is to have a trusted neutral arbiter who is well-versed in local custom to help decide what punishment is appropriate as victims may over-state their loss. Some punishment is necessary, even if it is not jail because without punishment, a criminal would steal with only the risk of making his victim "whole" if he were caught or the reward of the stolen goods if he were not.

driver who fails to properly set his brakes when parking or if a mechanic doesn't make the proper repair to a piece of machinery. If either of these situations results in someone being harmed, the truck owner or mechanic is responsible and must compensate the people they harmed.

But does negligence elevate to the level of a crime? Should a negligent person be punished similarly to a person *intentionally* violating consent? It could be argued that *repeated* negligent episodes could constitute criminality. But it would be difficult if not impossible to demonstrate an objective moment where negligence always becomes criminal.

Accidents

Often, consent is violated without any intent whatsoever. Jim is at a party when he kicks hit foot into a table and spills his glass of red wine all over Jill's white dress. Obviously, Jill didn't give Jim consent to stain her dress nor did Jim have any intention of staining it. Jim wasn't negligent; he was just being human.

Jim is still responsible even though it was neither a criminal act nor negligence. These are just situations that happen in the course of humans existing near one another. Depending on the situation, these kinds of events are nearly always resolved quickly; each person knows the circumstances, and the victim either simply waives it off or the offender offers a token of apology and an attempt to make the person whole by saying, "Please send me the cleaning bill."

To be perfectly consistent, Jim should also compensate Jill for the trouble of getting her dress cleaned and for its temporary loss of use. But many people understand that this is just a part of life and would prefer to live in a society where relatively harmless accidents are forgiven, knowing they also may commit them and appreciate *being* forgiven.

Risk

Intentionally taking an action that puts another person at a risk to which they did not consent is an aggression. However, there can be wide variances in the risk levels that people can impose onto others. The level of imposed risk determines whether any compensation is owed.

An airline introduces a new route, and airplanes are now flying at 35,000 feet over your house when they weren't before. This represents an extremely tiny additional risk to you. If you are in the slow lane on a freeway and a big rig passes you on the left, the truck driver is creating a small additional risk for you that wouldn't have been present had he not made that maneuver.

These risks, however, are the risks we all take simply by living life in a modern society. Planes flying overhead and driving on the road are risks we accept in our everyday lives with other people in a modern society. Because we accept them, such risks cannot be considered aggressions.

If someone gets behind the wheel after drinking alcohol rather than choosing to get a ride, that's an increased risk to you as another driver on the road, and it is an even greater risk if you are on the road in the same area at the same time. Shooting a gun in someone's direction is putting them at *significant* risk.

Therefore, at some point between flying a plane over a person's house at 35,000 feet and shooting at them, the risk imposed on the person without their consent changes from just the risk of living life to an aggression where the actor owes them compensation.

The argument behind compensating someone for exposed risk without consent — even if nothing bad happens — is based on the likelihood something bad *could have* happened. An example of how exposure to risk could be compensated is if Karl puts Lucas at a one-in-ten chance of being harmed without Lucas' consent, then by doing so, Karl owes Lucas one tenth of the compensation he would have owed had Lucas been physically harmed.

Obviously this is by no means a scientific method and can easily become unworkable. (How much does a drunk driver owe you exactly, if you were on the same road as them? What if you were a few blocks away from the driver at the time?) The point of this section is to show that people should be given the opportunity to express their consent before being exposed to undue risk.

Force and coercion

Intentionally limiting a person's agency using force or coercion can also be a violation of a person's consent. The use of explicit threats of violence, or credible implicit threats, limits a person's agency by introducing fear, which is one of life's strongest motivators. If a person uses the fear of harm or loss in order to force someone into taking an action (or to not act), they are committing an aggression against their target.

Acts intended to limit someone's agency without their consent can only be considered coercion when applied by another human being. Natural forces have no agency and therefore cannot violate consent. The argument that "a person is forced to work to eat or starve is therefore proof of their employer's evil coercion" is nonsense. Whether it's stocking shelves at a store, making deliveries, painting houses, farming the land, hunting, or fishing for one's own sustenance, *all human beings must work to survive*, and this biological requirement is not a violation of anyone's consent any more than it's a violation of consent that the sun is too hot for someone's liking. Only humans can coerce other humans.

Additionally, a coercing person must make an *illegitimate demand* against the target of the force. For example, in order for Mary to make an illegitimate demand of Nancy, Mary must make a demand for property she doesn't own (compensated or not) or require Nancy to take an action or refrain from taking an action. These are all an attempt by Mary to *assert control* over property Nancy has sole legitimate authority to control.

An illegitimate demand is necessary to establish coercion because a person who finds themselves in a bad situation *is not* being coerced by others who may end up benefiting from that situation (so long as those who benefit had no part in creating the situation itself).

If Olivia suddenly needed her car repaired but had no savings, her credit card company is not coercing her to borrow money to pay for it. If her employer required her to wear a uniform as a condition of working, the employer is not coercing her because she doesn't own the income stream they provide. (She doesn't have a legitimate authority to demand money unconditionally.) The income stream is given to her *in exchange* for her participation in the business's practices as defined by the individuals tasked with crafting them. She can choose to ignore those practices and not receive the income. If by making that choice she ends up being evicted from where she lives, the employer is not a party in that. They're no more responsible for her than any other employer. Olivia and her employer either engage in mutually voluntary trade (she performs the tasks the employer needs, the employer gives her money she needs) or they do not.

Compliance is not consent

Every day, peaceful individuals comply with countless aggressive acts taken against them to which they do not consent. They range widely in severity from someone cutting in line at a theme park to being compelled to undergo an invasive "pat-down" by a TSA agent to being robbed at gunpoint. In every case where a person's consent is violated, they must evaluate the cost of defending themselves and their property from the violator versus absorbing the cost of simply complying.

Within this cost consideration is also the prospect of preventing further violations. Social shaming of the line-jumper may be enough for him to embarrassingly leave the line entirely. Attempting to stop a TSA agent or street mugger would have significantly different outcomes if the attempt to stop them failed. (In the case of the TSA, you would likely have an even worse outcome if your attempt succeeded!)

Compliance is often *interpreted* as consent, especially by those who intend to harm others and later use the compliance of their victims as evidence of a consent signal. But regardless of the violation or any amount of resistance, *compliance in and of itself is not consent* as consent must always be explicitly given.

On this topic, some argue that compliance is still a *choice* or even that it's a *free choice*. This as a gross perversion of the concept of being "given" a choice. If a street mugger demands your money under threat of serious injury or death, he has actually *removed all but a few choices* from your life: run, fight, ignore, or comply. For most people there is really only one option. This is not being "given" choices but rather the opposite: being *forced* to make a choice from a small list of possible choices imposed onto the victim by the criminal.

Defensive action

Individuals always have the authority to defend themselves and their property against aggression initiated by others. This authority comes from the legitimate control we have over ourselves and our peacefully gained property — specifically, the authority to *exclude* others from ourselves and our property. The authority to exclude is the key ownership action we exercise when we physically defend our bodies or property from aggression.

These two concepts, exclusion from use and defensive action, go hand-in-hand. One cannot exist without the other. Without the authority to exclude others from use of your property (or yourself), you have no authority to stop an aggression. Conversely, if you are not allowed to stop an aggression, how can it be said that you have the authority to exclude them?

When taking defensive action, there can be a fine line between simply halting an aggression and initiating a *new* aggression. Only the *minimum amount of force required* to end an aggression may be employed. Once you stop an aggression against yourself or your property, using additional force against the initial aggressor may be considered a new aggression which could itself be defended.

If Suzanne attempts to give you a hug, for example, and you don't consent to it, you have the legitimate authority to physically prevent her from doing so. Putting your hands out or raising your forearms is usually sufficient to stop a friendly person who will respect your consent. But if Suzanne is an aggressive hugger, you may have to use more direct force to extract yourself from her clutches.

Regardless of how much force is required to halt her disrespect for your consent choice, if you were to then grab her purse and walk off with it, you would be committing a new aggression against *her*. Once Suzanne stopped her attempts to touch you, taking her purse would not be a necessary action because the aggression initiated against you had ended. Suzanne could then use the minimum physical force required to retrieve her purse.

Exceptions

Inability to consent

The most common situation that comes to mind when considering ability to consent is when a specific person does not have the physical ability to grant consent. This would be when a person is asleep, incapacitated, or otherwise not of a mental capacity to offer affirmative consent or to even understand what they are consenting to. Such deficiencies can be due to consuming drugs or alcohol, mental degeneration from age or disease, genetically limited cognitive ability, traumatic brain injury, or simply being a child. Under these circumstances there are a small set of specific moments when a presumption of granted consent exists. The scope of these situations is extremely narrow and all fall under the category of saving life or limb. An unconscious person who needs immediate medical care can generally be assumed to want to live, even in the case of attempted suicide where the person has specifically declared their intent. This last point is, admittedly, not always a straightforward call. Most people would agree that saving the life of teenager who attempted suicide even against their will is a good thing. (A stronger defense of overruling their non-consent to be saved is in the Children section.) But what about the 85-year-old who suffers from daily, incurable, excruciating pain? Who would be willing to stand guard to physically prevent a person in that situation from exercising one of their self-ownership powers?

Inability to withhold consent

Recall the principle of non-contradiction, that any argument or assertion in which a contradiction occurs cannot be correct. If Ruby and Eli were standing next to each other, and Ruby said, "It's a lovely day today," Eli cannot reasonably respond, "I never affirmatively consented to you saying that to me. You have violated my consent."

It may in fact be true that Eli didn't affirmatively consent to Ruby speaking those words. But there are two reasons why Ruby has not violated Eli's consent choices despite him not giving explicit affirmation for Ruby to speak:

1. It is not physically possible for Eli to grant explicit consent for the countless things Ruby could possibly say that he would not find objectionable.

2. Consent is universally human and applies to all people equally; i.e., the consent choices of each person are equally valid or invalid. Therefore, Ruby could immediately retort, "Well, *I* never affirmatively consented to *you* saying *that*, so *you* have now violated *my* consent!"

Item 2 in particular demonstrates the contradiction in attempting to restrict speech by withholding consent. If some speech could be considered a violation of consent, then the act of speaking to voice one's own objection could itself be a violation of another's consent, and so on. This is a nonsensical situation that clearly shows why speech (or any other peaceful communication or expression of ideas) cannot possibly be considered an aggression or a violation of consent — even if those ideas are abhorrent to us. Because the person who suggests that expressing an abhorrent idea is an aggression *could themselves be accused of committing an aggression by others.* It should be noted that a person screaming into your ear which could cause physical damage or someone preventing your movement to shove a picket sign in your face are examples of *actual* aggression.

Children

It is assumed throughout this book that the subjects who are granting and withholding consent are fully grown, independent adults who possess agency. Children, however, are in a separate category from adults, and even from other people of "reduced cognition." This is because childhood is universal: Every adult must have once been a child. All children (ideally) will eventually grow into their ability to consent and have the responsibility to respect others' consent. Nearly all children have a guardian who is expected to consent on their behalf. From even before birth through to adulthood, the guardian must consent to a great many things for the child. If children are not cared for to an equal or higher degree than guardians care for themselves, it can become a disaster for the family or worse if a culture of destructive "care" takes hold either through neglect or over-protection.

When can children make independent consent choices? It significantly depends on the child and the choice. The choice of what clothes they want to wear is much different from say, the choice to enter into a car loan. Setting an arbitrary age for any of these decisions is likely to be wrong for nearly every child. Some children are fully capable of understanding interest rates, penalties, and credit scores and have the maturity to commit to repay a loan at the age of 16. Others may not be ready for that transaction at 26.

There is an interesting dynamic in the parent/child relationship because of an important fact: Children are self-owning human beings just like adults. The parents, so long as the child is in their care, are not just expected but are in fact *obligated* to care for their child to the best of their ability. They are obligated not by society, culture, or any other external force; they are obligated by the *child herself as a self-owning person.*

The counterpart to such an obligation is the authority of the parents to consent and withhold consent *on behalf of* their child. Parents are given wide latitude in exactly when to give or withhold their child's consent and how they go about caring for their child. Parents have near complete control over which ideas and values are passed on to their child, so long as they are not being overtly physically or mentally abusive. Parents are granted near complete autonomy over their child's upbringing.[24]

---

24 What constitutes "abuse" is clearly subjective. Some believe teaching a religion is

The immediate objection is most commonly, "But how can caring for a child to the 'best of their ability' be an 'obligation?' Isn't that a clear violation of the *parents'* self-ownership to 'obligate' them to act a certain way? What if the parents decide to withhold their consent to care for their child?" This obligation is not a violation of the parents' consent because they can always voluntarily give up their parental duties to other people (i.e., give up the child for adoption) if they wanted to. Again, all humans can always revoke their consent at any time. The reason why they can't simply walk away from their baby is because the very act of walking away puts the child at risk of harm or death to which the child herself did not consent.

It is this combination, one of a self-owning human who will die without care and a caregiver who has the ability to voluntarily abdicate their role, that creates the requirement for the parents to give their best effort to raise a child so long as they remain in the caregiver role.

There is no section on abortion in this book.[25]

---

mental abuse; others feel similarly to teaching atheism. What is the difference between passing on your family's culture and brainwashing? Unfortunately, these topics are far beyond the scope of this book to explore and they don't relate to the link between consent and morality.

25 If you wish to guess what the author thinks, find the *objectively determinable* moment between conception and birth when self-ownership starts with the understanding that neither "viability" nor live birth are that moment. There is no discernible developmental change in a child that occurs during a trip down the birth canal, and "viability" is significantly a function of the technology available; humans do not suddenly own themselves earlier in the developmental cycle when a new medical technology is invented that can keep a baby alive.

5.
Morality

Morality — the consideration of "right" and "wrong" — is rooted in human agency (sometimes referred to as moral agency). Although the term "human agency" is occasionally used in a collective sense, such as "humanity's agency," this reference makes no sense. "Humanity" cannot act; only single individuals act. Therefore, "humanity" doesn't have agency. What appears to be the actions of "humanity," "the people," or "society" are in fact the combined effects of millions or billions of individuals acting by the force of their own will.

Because human beings have agency, they can choose to do harm or not do harm. Humans are not required to kill each other for resources; instead, we can form arguments, understand reason, and negotiate. The lion, as an example, has no such ability. Lions cannot decide to simply not hunt. They cannot negotiate with zebras for food. Therefore, they cannot be accused of "murdering" a zebra — or a human for that matter. Animals do not have agency because they do not choose their actions.[26] A human being can choose to go hungry instead of killing or stealing. An animal that operates on instinct alone cannot make such a choice.

Moreover, even a fully-functional human being is not considered to be acting immorally if their agency is removed from them without their consent. For example, a driver has her first seizure behind the wheel with no warning and no family history of seizures. If she crashes her car, the crash was not an immoral act. She was not negligent, and her actions were not intentional. The seizure caused the loss of her agency. Without agency, she cannot take the action necessary to prevent the crash. If she is physically unable to control her vehicle due to no fault of her own, any resulting crash cannot be immoral, as there was no *action*.

The ability to choose our own actions is our agency. It is agency that makes morality possible.

A chair has no agency. A book has no agency. A gun has no agency. Even an idea within a person's mind has no agency, nor does a person's speech. Agency resides within *each individual* to take *action* in order to bring thoughts or words into reality.

Only *human actions* can be viewed as moral or immoral.

Because agency exists only within humans, morality is a human construction. It is permanently linked to the human condition itself, and

---

26 Considering the intelligence of some species such as chimpanzees, gorillas, octopods, and dolphins, it's reasonable to ask when instinct ends and agency begins.

therefore it is not measured by any number of changing cultural norms. Any institution, ritual, or practice that exists within a culture is not itself a measure of morality. There is a clear separation between cultural norms and morality because institutions, rituals, and practices do not actually do anything; they are merely the *observation* of actions and behavior of individuals. Cultural norms and practices can *encourage* moral behavior or immoral behavior. For example, if people commonly praise those who give to charities, the cultural practice of praise will encourage more giving. If a cultural practice of, say, threatening people with physical violence *if they don't* give to charity developed, it would be an example of attempting to encourage moral behavior *using* immoral behavior. As mentioned previously, only an individual person acts. The praise or threats in the above examples are made by specific individuals. Only when acts are observed across multiple individuals can they be seen as cultural norms. Cultural norms, practices, or institutions cannot act.

Just as a thrown ball must be traveling either up or down or be stationary relative to the ground, each and every act must be moral, immoral, or amoral (neither moral nor immoral). No single act in one particular moment can be both moral and immoral simultaneously.

There could be situations where the same act would be moral if taken in one moment and immoral if taken the next moment. Driving through a busy intersection during a green light is a moral act. Driving through the same intersection a moment later when the light turns red is immoral due to the risk forced on other drivers without their consent. The same act could be moral if taken by one person and immoral if taken by another person. During a baseball game, the pitcher throwing a baseball toward the batter at high speed is a moral act. Someone in the stands throwing a baseball toward the batter at high speed is immoral because the batter has only consented to balls thrown at him by the pitcher. However, a single act taken at a single moment by a single person cannot be both moral *and* immoral as it would violate the principle of non-contradiction.

The morality of any act can also be heavily dependent upon the circumstances. If Jim smashes the window of a locked car, it can appear to be an immoral act because Jim is taking an ownership action (destruction) against another person's property without the owner's expressed consent. It seems perfectly clear that Jim's act is immoral until you discover there was a baby left in the car unattended.[27]

The point of this example is to show how the morality of an act can be judged differently depending on the view of the observer. The morality of each and every action can be judged from three separate vantage points:

1. The person who is taking the action

2. A person who is being acted against

3. An outside observer who neither acts nor is affected by the action

---

27 The assertion that sometimes there is a need to violate one person's consent in order to produce a much better outcome — or prevent a vastly worse outcome — needs careful exploration, which it receives in the section on moral dilemma examples.

Certainly there can be many different external observers to the same action. Billions of people can watch the same video of an action and have differing opinions regarding the morality or immorality of it. However, since one action cannot be both moral and immoral simultaneously, we must conclude that if there are multiple observers, and they disagree on whether a particular act is moral or not, then at least some of them are wrong.

Moreover, because outside observers were not involved with the action or its effects, they have no say whatsoever as to the "rightness" or "wrongness" of the action. They can certainly have and voice their opinion, but because no third party has the authority to consent or withhold consent regarding an action that doesn't affect them or their property, their opinion should be taken for what it's worth.

The actor clearly consents to taking the action. Being a self-owner with agency, the choice of taking an action *belongs to* the actor. If someone is being forced to take an "action" (either physically or through coercion), then the "actor" has no agency and therefore is not the one bringing the action into the world.[28]

But does the fact that the actor consents to taking their action speak to the *morality of the act itself*? It doesn't take long to think of examples of where an actor is doing something *they* believe is perfectly moral and "right," yet it is obvious to everyone else that what they are doing is actually evil. If those

---

28 If a big brother grabs his little brother's arm to make the little brother punch himself while saying, "Don't punch yourself," it isn't difficult to see who is using their agency.

who *take* actions against others were allowed to decide the morality of their actions, the world would be in a significantly worse place than it currently is. It's not clear if the human race could long survive with a societal rule that the actor determines their own right from wrong.

If neither the actor nor an observer can judge an act to be moral or immoral, we are left with only one possibility:

The *target* (i.e., the receiver) of an action is the only legitimate judge of an act's morality.

By definition, every person who does not consent to an action does not want that action taken against them. To withhold consent to an act you *want* makes no sense. To be clear, the word "want" is not being used as a replacement for "desire" or "wish," but as active *intent* for the recipient of the action. For example, a homeowner who desires to have her house painted may still not consent to a house painter offering to do the job if she doesn't have the money to pay for it right now. In this case, the owner withholds her consent until she can afford it. There is a very big difference between "wanting" something as in desiring it and "wanting" something as in, "I *want* you to show up at 8:00AM tomorrow to paint my house, and here is a contract that demonstrates my consent to compensate you for doing so."

All consent is given or withheld based on a large number of factors, time being one of them. What is acceptable now may not be in a day, or even one minute later. What is refused now could be cheerfully accepted at some later time.

If a person who withholds consent *does not* want an action to be taken, the person who grants consent *does* want the action to be taken (or at the very least is amenable to it). This presents us with an opportunity to recognize and eliminate a contradiction:

> **No one can both give consent to and withhold consent from a person acting against them at the same time. If they could, this would mean they both accept and do not accept the action being taken which is a contradiction.**

Because we know that giving consent to an action demonstrates it's either wanted or accepted and that withholding consent demonstrates it is neither a wanted nor accepted action, it's clear that from the point of view of the person making the consent choice that the action in question is *seen to them* as being either "good" or "bad" (i.e., "moral" or "immoral") given all the circumstances they are evaluating.

But if different people would either consent or withhold consent to the exact same act, even given the same circumstances, doesn't that mean that morality is in fact subjective to each person and is therefore not able to be connected to an objective, human-wide measure?

No, it does not. There is a "higher level" concept above the acts themselves. This will be explored in a later section.

What morality is not

Before that "higher level" concept is covered, a few concepts that are commonly and mistakenly compared to morality should be discussed.

Legality

It is sometimes claimed the rules and legislation that exist in most Western societies (referred to as a "legal framework") are an extension of a moral code. That collective, democratic action of "the people" makes these rules moral.[29]

In fact, modern legal frameworks in Western societies are almost entirely uncoupled from morality. There are a few actions considered illegal that are also immoral. But every other law is at best a rule that is discovered and documented by neutral arbiters during the process of resolving conflicts, very similar to how the rules of language are discovered and documented. At worst, laws are arbitrary rules that serve the very people who create, maintain, and enforce them.

When discussing matters of consent and morality, artificial "entities" that are created under an invented legal framework (such as corporations and government agencies) can be confusing. Great care must be taken to fully separate the discussion of legal entities from the discussion of actual human

---

29 "Morality and Democracy" Emile Boutroux, The North American Review vol. 214 No. 789 (Aug. 1921), pages 166-176 https://www.jstor.org/stable/251207

beings. Legal entities are all a convenient fiction, sometimes used for human benefit and other times to human detriment.

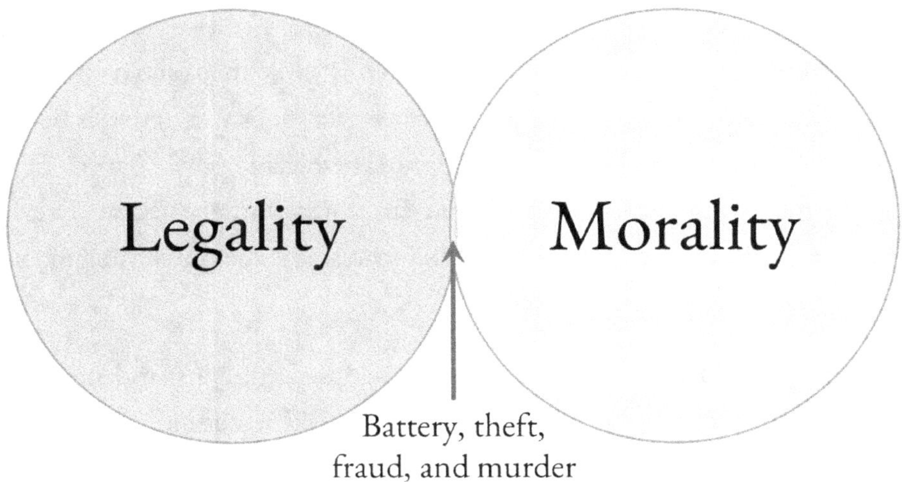

A handy Venn diagram that shows where the worlds of legality and morality intersect.

Corporations

While it is indeed convenient to refer to a company as a person in the sense that "the company owns the building," it's confusing and misleading to believe a company — or a corporation — is a person.

Companies themselves are not people and as such they do not have agency. Companies are merely a vehicle by which multiple individuals can pool their resources to attain greater ends than they could separately. They are essentially legal contracts. For example, an ownership contract might state, "If you own 1,000 shares of the company, you will receive 0.1% of dividends as declared by vote of the top 10 shareholders." Essentially, companies are mutual agreements. You are not forced to enter the contract (which is accomplished by simply not buying the shares). Once entered, however, the unanimous agreement by all shareholders is while they each own a tiny slice of the value of any property (money, physical goods, etc.) that is being controlled by the company, they have limited ownership power over it. This agreement is completely consensual and therefore voluntary because to exit the agreement, all one must do is sell the shares. It is the purchasing of the shares that *is* the explicit consent.

However, separating ownership from individual humans and creating an entity that can "own" things invites the risk of conflict within the organization of who exactly has control as, again, companies don't act, only humans act.[30]

Public Property

While the existence of companies (a centrally-managed set of pooled resources) can confuse the idea of ownership by being referred to as people when they themselves are not people, even more confusing is the concept of "public property."

---

30 Do *not* confuse the fact that a corporation is not a person with the valid decision to give an *actual person* legitimate authority (as authorized by the legitimate owners) to act on behalf of the owners and use the resources of the corporation in a manner that follows the owners' wishes. To use force in an attempt to stop the pooling of resources in this way would be a direct violation of the owners' consent choices.

As discussed, only the *legitimate* owner of a property (one who has acquired it peacefully and through voluntary exchange) has the authority to take ownership actions. Among these actions is the authority to exclude others from its use. In modern Western societies, governments claim this authority over what they deem to be "public property."

The idea that "the public" (meaning every person in a specific geographic zone) "owns" some particular property is to say *every person in that zone* has a legitimate authority to exclude other people from that property. But the very idea of "public property" is that *no one* has the authority to exclude others (i.e., "everyone" can use it). This is a clear contradiction. For example, supposedly anyone can walk on a public beach. Anyone can enter and use a public park. It's well known, however, that government can close a "public" beach or "public" park at their discretion or physically remove someone for bad behavior. How is this different from a shopping mall where "everyone" is assumed to be allowed to enter? Shopping malls are owned by one organization, and it's reasonable to understand the mall can dictate its own closing time, or even close for no reason at all, and eject unwanted individuals.

Therefore the idea of "public" property is merely a euphemism. It's much more accurate to say that these things are "government property"[31] as

---

31 Astute readers will know that government agents don't merely claim authority to exclude people from "public" property but also from individually owned (private) property as well under circumstances government actors themselves have defined. This is further explored in a later section.

government certainly *claims* to have the authority to exclude whom they wish to exclude, even if most of the time they generously allow "the public" to use the property.

Ethics

It is common for people to use the words "morals" and "ethics" interchangeably. This causes unnecessary confusion which can be reduced by separating the concepts.

While morality is based entirely on human agency, ethics develop culturally. Morality is found inside the human actor. Ethics can be defined as rules of conduct people are expected to follow which are *imposed by others*. This proposed difference between morality (as judged by the individual receiver of an action) and ethics (as judged by people other than those involved with an action) creates a clear-cut delineation which makes communication on these topics much easier.

Professional organizations create ethical rules (sometimes implicitly, sometimes explicitly) to guide those doing business within the profession in a positive manner. Following ethical rules ensures the long-term stability of the profession. It builds trust and mutual understanding between the provider of services and their clients. For instance, the elimination of conflict of interest is one type of ethical requirement in many professional organizations.[32]

---

32 https://ethicsunwrapped.utexas.edu/glossary/conflict-of-interest

However, ethical codes can differ widely between groups and professions. The very same act that would violate one profession's ethical code could be perfectly acceptable or even expected in other groups. As a stark example, it's a serious ethical violation for a therapist to have an affair with her client. But whether you agree or disagree with the idea of legal brothels, given that they exist, it is certainly *not* an ethical violation for a worker at a brothel to sleep with *her* client.

There are even ethical rules that guide social behavior such as attending a wedding without a gift, showing up to a dinner party without a bottle of wine, or leaving a friend's home immediately after eating a meal.

Ethics describe what is expected of you *by* others.

6.
Consent is Equivalent to Morality

When considering a universal equivalence of consent and morality, it's necessary to think about actions and consent on three separate levels. The first level is where we find the *actual acts* people take in their raw form. Actions are the measurable reality of one human being's physical manifestation of their agency. Examples would be using violence against another person, taking another person's property, ingesting drugs or drinking,

The first level is the physical action of an individual that could be moral or immoral.

giving another person a hug, or getting a tattoo. In other words, the first level of understanding is the real-life actions a person takes that other people will be judging as moral or immoral.

The second level is how each person would choose to consent to, or withhold consent from, each action. Every single person on Earth has a somewhat different view of when they would consent to any particular act, even if they would consent to it at all. Looking at each of the previous examples, it's easily imagined that very few people would consent to being punched. By contrast, many people would consent to receiving a hug, but then again, fewer would consent to receiving a hug from a stranger. Some people consider drugs, alcohol, and tattoos as inherently immoral in and of themselves and so would consider anyone involved with their sale, possession, or use as acting immorally.

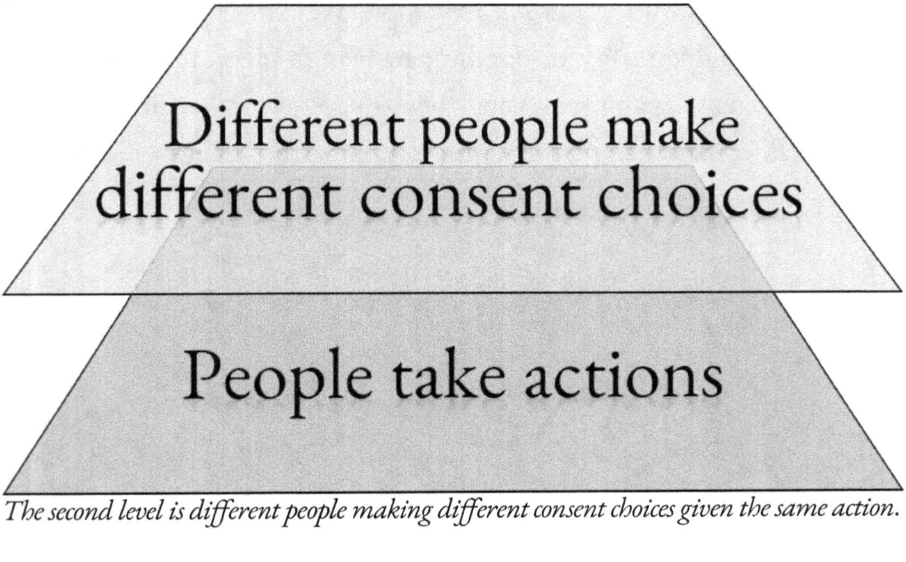

Different people make
different consent choices

People take actions

The second level is different people making different consent choices given the same action.

This is where people often stop in their evaluation. People naturally decide what is moral or immoral based on what *they themselves* would do. Viewing the world from this level results in different incorrect conclusions depending on how much hubris the person has. Let's take two people, Lisa and Mark:

Mark always "knows" which actions are moral and which actions are immoral. He is informed by his religion or by some other ideology which he assumes is infallible. He simply judges the actions of others against what *he* would consent to, basing his judgment on his ideology which he assumed to be correct to begin with. This is known as a begging the question fallacy.[33] According to this fallacy, he believes he is always correct about what is moral and immoral *because* the ideology he bases his beliefs on is always correct about what is moral and immoral.[34]

Lisa, on the other hand, as she looks around and sees everyone having a different view of morality, concludes that *morality itself* is really up to each individual to discover on their own terms. This may bring Lisa to the belief that morality is subjective. After all, each human makes subjective choices about what they believe is moral, so she comes to believe that morality itself can never be concretely defined. Furthermore, when she starts thinking about how the actions people consent to can be different as cultural norms change, that makes it all the more apparent to her that morality is malleable.

---

33 https://www.logicallyfallacious.com/logicalfallacies/Begging-the-Question

34 Mark can overcome his fallacy by first proving his ideology is correct without using the ideology itself in his proof.

But neither Mark nor Lisa has arrived at the correct conclusion because they are not considering the next level of logic beyond what they plainly observe. As discussed, the first level is the specific actions people take against others. At the second level, people affected by those acts (those who were acted against) will either consent or withhold consent based on their own viewpoint and circumstances. But regardless of the act and regardless of the affected person's views, like all other people, they do in fact either give consent or withhold consent.

This is the third level: For *every single action* taken against *every single person*, the one who is being acted against *always* either consents to or does not consent to that action. As stated previously, there can be no situation where consent is both given and withheld. There can also be no situation where consent is neither given nor withheld, because unless consent is affirmatively given, it is by definition withheld. Therefore:

All human beings either consent to or do not consent to every single action taken against them.

This is the *universality* of consent. The person's background, their momentary conditions, their history, and their future intent are all totally irrelevant to the absolute and objective fact that they have either consented to or not consented to the action.

It's not about the actions people take (the first level), and it's not about how different people would or would not consent to the same action (the second level), it's about the fact that *everyone who is the target of an action either consents or does not consent.*

The third level is all people always make a consent choice for each and every action.

This fact is almost too simple. It's so simple one could be forgiven for mistaking it for a tautology. But it is this critical understanding that is the link between consent and morality and why they are equivalent.

In the section describing the equivalence principle, we learned that when two things are indistinguishable from one another, they are said to be equivalent. The person who was inside the "enclosed room" saw his world objectively, with no ability to see things outside his room. His own view of his own universe, regardless of how others may be seeing his "universe" from the outside, is true and correct for him. Recall also that there could be other, outside observers who would *completely disagree* with what the person in the room was experiencing and that this disagreement between the internal and external observer did not negate the fact that the person in the room *cannot distinguish* between acceleration and gravity — in other words, seeing them as equivalent.

When a person makes a consent choice, they are observing the universe from their own "enclosed room" of their own mind.

The individual who is affected by an act evaluates their environment and makes a consent choice. Someone outside their mind — an external observer — may see the environment differently. But again, this difference in viewpoint carries no weight to the fact that the affected person did in fact choose one way or another.

Within the mind of every single person, they have either consented to an action taken against them or they have not. If they have not consented (i.e., if their consent was violated) then their view is the act itself was immoral or "wrong."

Because each person within their mind equates respecting their consent choice as a moral act and violating their consent as an immoral act, each person equates consent with morality. And the fact that other people would consent to things differently *has no bearing on the fact that they themselves also equate respect for their own consent choices with morality.*

The equivalence principle holds:

Because all individuals equate acceleration with gravity, regardless of the views of others, then acceleration and gravity are, in a very real sense, equivalent.

Because all individuals equate consent with morality, regardless of the views of others, then consent and morality are, in a very real sense, equivalent.

An Alternative Approach

There is an additional, albeit simpler way to see the connection between consent and morality.

Take a few moments and think of as many wrong acts as you can...

- Taking someone's property

- Physically harming someone

- Deceiving someone in a trade (fraud)

- Putting someone at risk of harm

Once you have these in mind, it becomes clear that there are always exceptions to these acts. The same acts aren't *always* immoral given a different situation...

- Giving permission to take the property

- Undergoing invasive surgery

- Deciding to gamble knowing the casino has an unstated advantage

- Running a sky-diving business

What is it about these exceptions that turn a wrong act into an act that is not immoral at all? The common trait is consent. Every exception to the immorality of harming another person comes from consent of the person being "harmed."

7.
Moral Dilemma Examples

It would be foolish to suggest that any theory on morality could be perfect in all possible cases, especially when creatures as imperfect and versatile as human beings are involved. The creation of a complete theory to solve all situations is impossible. There will always be examples found that are simply not solvable within the system.

Considering this limitation, here are some dilemmas posed to those who hold the idea that self-ownership, property ownership, consent, and morality are closely tied. Note that these are not *ethical* dilemmas, which are tied to behavior within social and workplace settings. (Take for one instance the psychiatrist whose patient reveals their desire to commit a murder. Setting aside any legal requirements to report it, should they inform the potential target?) The scenarios in this section attempt to push boundaries and test the resiliency of the link between consent and morality.

Example 1: The "Hot Air Balloon" Problem

The hot air balloon problem explores the limits of property ownership authority. The general assertion concerning property is that separate legitimate interests in property cannot conflict. For example, if I am sitting in your car, even though I am a self-owner, only you, the owner of the car, have the legitimate authority to consent to its use. If you did not consent to me being in your car, you are morally permitted to physically remove me from it if I refuse to respect your consent choice. In other words, my self-ownership claim doesn't grant me authority to violate your legitimate ownership authority over your car. Your act of removing me is legitimate because I have committed an act (of getting into your car without your consent) which is illegitimate.

To explore this further, say you get into the basket of your hot air balloon. You lift yourself and your balloon to an altitude of 1,000 feet, at which point you discover that I (somehow) sneaked into the basket as you took off without you noticing. The basket is your property. You did not consent to my being in the basket, so my act is most definitely a consent violation by me against you.

Question: Are you, as in the case of the car, morally permitted to physically remove me from the basket, knowing that doing so would guarantee my death?

There are highly esteemed thinkers who would argue that yes, you are morally permitted to remove me, the trespasser, as the consequences of such an eviction should have been reasonably known to me, and that you are not, in fact, killing me, but that the natural force of gravity is doing the "killing."[35]

This argument is not compelling. As a human being, you have agency. You can choose whether to evict me or not evict me. In this example, if it is asserted that I should be expected to understand the consequences of trespassing in a balloon, then you should also be expected to understand the consequences to me of throwing me out of it. Stated differently, if we expect a trespassing stowaway to know that being removed from the balloon will kill him, and therefore should have understood death was a possibility, then the balloon owner *should also* be expected to know that evicting a stowaway is the same as sentencing him to death.

Because you have full knowledge that evicting me from your balloon would guarantee my death, and because you have agency, physically evicting me from the basket at 1,000 feet is *morally equivalent* to simply killing me where I stand and then dumping me overboard. Therefore, when the problem is properly understood, the real question is:

---

35 https://findwords.info/term/evictionism

Is death the appropriate punishment for someone who is merely trespassing?

The answer is no. Trespassing certainly is an aggression. However, a property owner is only permitted to use the *minimum necessary* force in order to end the aggression.[36] You as the balloon owner have no more authority to punish my trespass with a life-ending eviction any more than a homeowner has the authority to shoot anyone who happens to walk on their front lawn.[37]

There's another way to illustrate why the assertion that "nature is doing the killing, not me" argument is wrong. Using a different example, remove the balloon from the scenario and assume you are peacefully sitting in your own home. I come busting into your home uninvited, and although I am a trespasser, I'm not there to harm you or steal anything from you. I am merely seeking safety from an angry mob that is out to kill me.

You look out your front window, and indeed there is a mob of people demanding that I be removed from your property so they can administer their mob justice against me. You have no knowledge of the backstory, only that the people in the mob have decided to respect your property and ask only that you evict me as is your right as the property owner.

---

36 As discussed in the Defensive Action portion of the Consent section.

37 There are an infinite number of variations of trespass including those where implied threats of violence exist, such as someone entering your home without your consent. The hot air balloon example is meant to examine a simple trespass situation where no other threats are present.

Question: Are you morally permitted to physically remove me from your home knowing that doing so would guarantee my death?

But hold on a moment. Is this really the same as the balloon situation? It's true that I am trespassing and that evicting me seems pretty certain to make today my last day. But there is a very big difference: The individuals in the mob *have agency* whereas Earth's gravity *does not*. A flying bullet has no agency. Only the shooter has agency. Natural forces like gravity have no agency. The person pushing someone from a great height *does* have agency.

In this example, it would not be immoral to evict me. Your eviction would not decide my fate as it did in the balloon; it's the *people in the mob* who are deciding it.[38]

Example 2:
Falling Off the Balcony

You're enjoying a view from your 15th floor apartment balcony when you lose your footing and tumble over the edge. By sheer luck, the apartment owner below you on the 14th floor has a flagpole which you grab onto in order to save your life.

---

38 Use this logic the next time you see a movie where a kidnapper says something like, "Meet my demands or I'll kill the hostage, and her blood will be on your hands!" No. It's always critical to know who is using their agency to harm others. The person most culpable for harming others is the person who is actually harming others.

The flagpole owner notices you and says, "Excuse me, but that flagpole is my property. You are trespassing and must let go."

You take a moment and ask yourself if you should you respect this person's ownership authority, let go, and fall to your death, or do you violate their consent and save yourself? As a moral purist you immediately decide on the correct course of action and pull yourself onto their balcony.

As a trespasser you most certainly are committing an aggression. You are intentionally violating their explicit withholding of their consent for which you owe some level of compensation, even if that compensation is a simple apology. Can the flagpole owner now just push you off the balcony to halt your transgression? As we learned in the Defensive Action section and the hot air balloon example above, only the minimum force required to halt an aggression is permissible before the defensive action itself becomes a new aggression. Fortunately, the 14th floor resident needs only to apply enough force to open their front door so you can walk out.

Example 3:
Violating Consent for the "Greater Good"

The next three scenarios test the idea that taking or destroying another person's property without their consent is still a "moral" act when the outcome for doing so either results in the furtherance of a greater good or the prevention of a greater tragedy. The scenarios differ slightly from each other, but they are good illustrations of the nature of consent in extreme circumstances as seen from different viewpoints.

Scenario A: The boy who fell in the lake

Say you're walking along the shore of a lake. You look out and see a child by himself on an inflatable raft. You witness the child fall into the lake with no life preserver. Every attempt by the child to grab the raft merely pushes it away. You know he will soon tire and drown if help doesn't reach him quickly.

You indeed quickly find a man with a motorboat tied to a dock that could reach the child in moments. Shockingly, he's not willing to untie his boat and save the child. You offer to do it if he would simply lend you the boat. He refuses. Noting to yourself that people in moral quandary puzzles tend to be jerks, you offer $1,000 to rent his boat for five minutes to save the child. To your dismay, the owner refuses again.

> **Question: Are you morally permitted to take the boat in violation of its owner's consent in order to save the child?**

If you chose to take the boat, you would indeed be violating the owner's consent. There is no "because you're a jerk" exception to his self-ownership or his ownership authority over the boat. If you took the boat, you would be stealing it.

Though few people would support punishing you for taking the boat, you still have the boat owner to contend with. If he chose to defend his property, he would be morally permitted to defend his boat with the minimum force necessary (which may include physical force) to stop you from taking it.[39]

Assuming you were able to escape with the boat and save the child, you would need to return the boat to its rightful owner. As a thief, you are required to make the boat owner whole as well as receive a punishment for your intentionally criminal act. Having made the voluntary choice to steal a boat to save a life, likely you feel whatever punishment you must now receive will be worth it.

This scenario appears to justify taking an action that harms one person so long as the action serves the "greater good." However, a person who held themselves to the principle of not violating others' consent would indeed be *violating their own principles* if they stole the boat.[40]

Undoubtedly most people would sympathize with your action in this hyper-rare scenario. Because you decided to take the action of stealing the boat upon yourself, *you* took the risk of being violently stopped by the boat

---

39 This is only the case if the boat owner had no part or responsibility for the child or his predicament. If the boat owner was the father of the child or had intentionally or negligently placed the child in the high-risk situation of being in an unstable raft with no life preserver (a violation of the child's consent), he would have no authority to withhold his consent from someone acting to remove the risk *he* was responsible for generating. For the purposes of this example, the boat owner is not responsible for the child.

40 An interesting exercise for the reader: If a person is willing to violate their own principles in this arbitrary scenario, where should they draw the line? What level of harm is worth inflicting on peaceful yet unwilling people in order to mitigate another person's risk?

owner, and you were willing to *personally bear the punishment* for your theft and then make the owner whole according to local norms. The willingness to bear personal responsibility for one's own actions is absent in the next scenario which examines a situation significantly more common than a boat owner unwilling to help save the life of a child.

This next scenario may be challenging for many people. The importance of *every human being* deserving to have their consent choices respected must always be kept in mind while considering the ideas being presented.

Scenario B: The homeless person and the billionaire

In Scenario A, a person took a boat without the owner's consent and used it to save a child's life. How is this any different from taking money from a billionaire and giving it to a homeless person who is at imminent risk of dying as well?

The notion in modern Western societies that a very rich person must give up a portion of their property for the benefit of others (who did not offer any goods or services in trade for it) isn't merely common, it is ubiquitous.

But there is an important difference between these two scenarios. In Scenario A, everyone knows it is a violation of consent to take the boat. Everyone knows that taking the boat is committing the crime of theft. Everyone knows that consequences in the form of compensation and punishment must be paid by the individual person who takes the boat without permission. It was *your personal decision* in Scenario A to act in that extreme moment. Because you made a personal choice to steal the boat, you accepted the consequences of that act as a personal cost to you. In Scenario B, however, the billionaire is not being coerced to give up some of his money by any single individual. He is being coerced by a giant organization of people, some of whom carry firearms.

So that there is no ambiguity: *Under no circumstances can taking property by use of coercion be justified as a moral act.*

Using coercion to get an owner to agree to give up their property is morally indistinguishable from simply taking their property. Both are violations of consent. Both are the crime of theft.

The use of credible threats of violence in order to coerce a human being into handing over their property is the crime of theft. There is no "because I really need it" exception to theft. There is no "because you can afford it" exception to theft. There is no "because I have no other idea how to accomplish my goals" exception to theft.

As mentioned earlier, *actors cannot decide* the morality of their actions. The fact that the actor does not personally believe there is anything wrong with using coercion to take property without the owner's consent (regardless of any future benevolent use for what is taken) doesn't change an immoral act into a moral act. If a person must be coerced to give up their property, then they do not consent because no one who consents must be coerced. Theft is *always* an aggression. Theft is *always* immoral.

As an extreme example, if it could somehow be mathematically proven that the prosperity level of the United States in the 1860s was measurably higher with slavery than it would have been without slavery, would you call for the repeal the 13th Amendment?[41] What if *the only way* poor children at that time could afford clothing was due to the slave labor used to provide the raw material to make it? Would you then advocate for the U.S. government to provide a slavery apparatus today? Doesn't the enslavement of the few for the benefit of others serve "the greater good?"

Of course it doesn't. We intuitively understand that it is immoral to extract value from others using violent force (slavery) even if that value is used by those who desperately need it. While it can be argued that taking people's property isn't "*as* criminal" as entirely enslaving a person, as discussed previously, taking their property is no different from taking the portion of their life spent creating the value of that property. Stealing someone's property is equivalent to a temporary slavery.

The only time it is a moral act to take someone's property is if the property itself was obtained by that person illegitimately (such as through theft, fraud, or coercion). Even then, the only one who deserves to receive that property is the *original person from which it was taken*. If a particular billionaire never directly violated anyone's consent, how can it be said

---

41 This is merely a thought experiment and *not* the author's position. The United States was poorer than it would have been due to the use of slavery and became more prosperous after its abolition. https://www.econlib.org/archives/2014/09/ending_slavery.html

that his property was illegitimately gained from victimizing a particular poor person?

In the case of Scenario B, it could be reasonably argued that entire systems are in place (such as the U.S. Federal Reserve, for example) to enrich the billionaire *at the expense* of poor individuals, even if the billionaire did not directly steal from or otherwise victimize any particular person. A real and existing system by which some individuals gain at the expense of others could itself be a consent violation. It's doubtful there are any rational people who would knowingly agree to be impoverished just so a few others they never met could become unimaginably wealthy. Even if such systems could be immediately abolished, righting previous wrongs from them would prove to be impossibly complex.

At the risk of getting derailed, it's worth taking a moment to explore *why* making a billionaire's supposed "victims" whole may be impossible. The first challenge is finding out who exactly perpetrated the violation of consent. (Is it the people in the U.S. Federal Reserve? Is it the people writing laws that enable the rich while disabling the poor? Is it the people who enforce those laws? Who, precisely, are the violators?) Even then, can it be reasonably expected of someone who has worked within a system well-established before they were born to know that the *system itself* was created in violation of others' consent? Perhaps there is culpability to be found with the creators of the immoral system *and* the billionaire who profited from its use, but they may not be equally blame-worthy, and the most culpable people may have died a long time ago.

The second challenge is determining *precisely how much* the billionaire gained directly because of the immoral (consent-violating) acts of those who run the existing system. Any wealth the billionaire made through mutually voluntary action is *not* subject to be "returned" to anyone; only that which was taken illegitimately (along with what would make any victims whole).

The third, fourth, and fifth challenges are to determine *precisely who* was victimized, *how much* they were deprived of, and exactly what compensation would make them whole. Any deviation from accurately finding these three values would result in a new victimization. It seems clear that the challenges in this complicated scenario are simply impossible to resolve. Any attempt to do so would almost certainly result in even worse outcomes.[42]

Scenario C: A baby locked in a car on a hot day

While walking across a giant parking lot on a hot summer day, you notice a baby strapped into the back seat of a locked car. The engine is turned off and the owner is nowhere in sight. Considering that you do not have the expressed consent of the car's owner, breaking the window would normally be a violation of their ownership authority.

But unlike in the case of the boat owner, the car owner *is in fact responsible* for placing the child in a life-threatening situation. While the owner of the

---

42 Any person placed in charge to find these values for hundreds of millions of people would invariably succumb to additional pressures from those who stand to benefit from the new situation. The likely best option is to simply end the current immoral system that enables ongoing violations of consent.

boat had his property taken without having committed any aggression against anyone, the car owner most certainly has committed an aggression; they have put a self-owning human at significant risk without that human's consent. Considering the car owner is not in close proximity to the car (and so is unable to unlock it for you) and there is a helpless self-owning person at extreme risk of death, the car owner *has no* authority to withhold consent from your breaking their window. Moreover, where the boat owner deserves compensation, the car owner is owed nothing from you breaking their window as they were the cause of the situation, even if the child was put in danger unintentionally.

Example 4: Two innocent property owners

This example stems from the one in the Crimes section. In that example, a car thief stole your car and hid it in his garage. It was demonstrated that he did not have the authority to withhold his consent from you (or someone on your behalf) taking the minimum amount of destructive action necessary to retrieve your legitimately-owned property.

What if the thief parked your car not in his own garage but in his *mother's* garage without telling her? She is completely innocent in the matter. She is under no obligation to even look in her garage much less let you into it. She has not committed an aggression against you in any way.

Under normal, everyday circumstances, peaceful people have no desire to deprive other peaceful people of what is rightfully theirs. When a child accidentally kicks a ball into their neighbor's yard, most people happily return it. This is the ideal society that most of us want to live in.

So long as the mother is unknowingly harboring stolen property, she is blameless. As mentioned previously, intent is the factor that governs the difference between an innocent, negligent, or criminal violation of consent. In a situation where she not only doesn't know your consent was violated but *couldn't* know (because her son placed your car into her garage without her knowledge), then it's impossible for her to have any culpability in the crime because she had no agency in the situation. She was never able to make a voluntary choice of whether or not to keep your car in her garage.

There is a very simple solution to this problem: Inform the mother that your property is in her garage. Once she is made aware that she is in possession of your property, she has full agency to make a specific choice: either allow you, the rightful owner, to take your property back or prevent you from accessing your property.

If she then chooses to refuse you access to your property by use of her agency — an active choice of hers which is not being coerced — she is now intentionally violating your withheld consent to exclude herself from your property. You are then morally justified in taking the minimum necessary action to retrieve your property as you did in the previous example.

8.
How This Can Change the World

This book is specifically meant for people who already understand that forcing others to choose or do something they do not wish to choose or do is wrong. It is meant for those who intuitively know that the ability to express consent choices and have them be respected is what *all* peaceful people deserve.

This section is for people who want nothing less than to place the morality of consent front-and-center in their society in order to create a better, more peaceful world. Discussed here are the serious problems that arise when a society (such as the current Western society) departs from keeping the respect of consent among its highest ideals.

If that interests you, then you cannot be afraid to explore the dark taboos of forbidden topics; you must be willing to "slay sacred cows." You must also be willing to reject many ideas that are deeply ingrained in the minds of most other people. You must be willing to face your own contradictions and be capable of accepting what could prove to be a major shift in your own worldview. Only then can you join a growing chorus of moral consistency and be part of the solution to the great social problems caused by the widespread disrespect of consent choices.

The Problem

Do you believe in the primacy of respecting consent? Do you believe the act of intentionally violating a peaceful person's consent is immoral or sometimes even criminal *regardless of who does it?* Do you believe all peaceful people are equally deserving of having their consent choices respected? Then there is only one question to ask:

> **Why do you feel the need to impose your beliefs onto others by force?**

This is a very challenging question for most people to answer honestly. Most everyone sees themselves as a positive, respectful person who never would willingly impose their views onto others. And through the daily course of their lives, they regularly live up to those ideals.

But what the overwhelming majority of people in Western societies don't realize is that they participate or believe in a system which imposes decisions onto many other people without any regard for the consent choices of other people.

This is your challenge: You know it is not permissible to impose your choices onto other people. You know it is immoral to use threats of violence to coerce others to follow rules you may even believe to be beneficial to everyone.

And then...

    ... on one special day ...

        ... every couple of years ...

You along with millions of other people cast a vote and together choose rules, rulers, and rule-makers everyone else must live with.[43] You participate in the choosing of individuals (politicians) *knowing full well* they will force their ideas onto others who have not given their consent.

As discussed earlier, outside of certain specific exceptions, *no person can consent for another person.* Alicia cannot consent for Betty. This limitation goes for more than simple things like the use of Betty's property. While Alecia can certainly consent to rules created by Chris if she wishes, Alecia cannot declare that *she and Betty* will both follow the rules created by Chris without a previous agreement with Betty.

---

43 If you honestly believe you are not making a choice for everyone else but merely "making your voice heard," then you may wish to ponder this question and answer it honestly: If your vote was the only vote (or you knew yours was the deciding vote), would you still cast your ballot? If the answer is yes, then your intent is in fact to impose your will onto others. If the answer is no, then why are you casting a ballot in the first place?

After all, what exactly *is* an election? An election is merely a popularity contest held by and very tightly controlled by the very organization it is supposed to hold accountable. Consider the following:

Who *counts* the votes? **Who** *declares* the winner? **Who** decides *when* you vote? **Who** decides *how often* you vote? **Who** makes the rules on *who* can vote? **Who** makes rules on *how to enter* a race? **Who** chooses what you *wear* when you vote? **Who** decides how vote controversies are resolved? **Who** decides if you're allowed to vote on new rules?[44] **Who** chooses which contests you're allowed to vote in?[45] **Who** makes rules on how candidates can communicate with the voters? **Who** decides which new rules are put up for a vote? **Who** can nullify votes if *they decide* the outcome violates one of *their own* rules? **Who** will physically put their hands on you and lock you in a jail cell if you break one of their rules about the vote?

It's the government, of course — the people who are themselves affected by the outcome of the vote.[46] Who would consent to giving any organization

---

44 Whether or not individuals are allowed to vote on specific rules (such as propositions) is governed by laws made by government legislatures.

45 Government actors decide what district you're in and will adjust them to suit their own purposes. See: https://www.washingtonpost.com/news/wonk/wp/2015/03/01/this-is-the-best-explanation-of-gerrymandering-you-will-ever-see/

46 As established, only individuals act. Organizations such as corporations and governments themselves do not act. Having said that, it is much easier to explain the points in this section by referring to acts committed by government agents and employees as being "government acts." In this section, it should be assumed that a "government

this much control over the very process intended to keep it in check? The idea that elections hold government actors accountable while government actors completely control every rule surrounding elections is ludicrous on its face.

"The consent of the governed" (as popularized by the *Declaration of Independence*[47]) can't actually exist unless each and every "governed" person consents — and then never chooses to withhold their consent later on. *No human can consent for another human.* Just because a government actor publicly announces that the majority of those who participated in a vote between Person A and Person B *really did* choose Person A, exactly how does that give Person A an authority (to create rules and enforce them) that he never had and that none of the people who voted for him have?

Additionally, just because someone is being *offered* the opportunity to participate in an election does not mean they consent to its result. If Allison were to offer you a vote between buying vanilla or chocolate ice cream, and you choose neither flavor, you haven't consented for Allison to force you to buy what she chooses.

---

act" is an act taken by a person who self-identifies as a government agent or employee, primarily including (but not limited to) elected politicians, their staff, regulatory bodies, law enforcement, judges (elected or appointed), prosecutors, and any local agencies such as DMVs, Social Services, public schools, etc.

47 https://www.archives.gov/founding-docs/declaration-transcript

People can grant only their own authority to others

You have complete authority to consent to acts others take which directly affect you or your legitimate property. This means you can also *transfer that authority* to others. Some examples of transferring authorities:

- Because you have the authority to move yourself from one place to another, you can authorize a ride share service to take you there.

- Because you have the authority to defend yourself, you can authorize a bodyguard to defend you.

- Because you have the authority to make end-of-life decisions for yourself, you can authorize a family member to make them for you in the event you are unable to.

However, you have no authority to violate the consent of others. Therefore:

- You cannot authorize your driver to hit people who are in your way.

- You cannot authorize your bodyguard to attack or otherwise initiate violence against others.

- You cannot authorize your family members to make end-of-life decisions for other people.

Yet millions of people believe the simple act of marking a vote on a piece of card stock printed with someone's name on it somehow enables them to grant the individual named on that card special powers that the voters themselves neither possess nor have the authority to grant.

No individual can legitimately grant to someone else an authority which they do not first possess.

It is widely believed the activity of holding an election *is the* mechanism by which certain individuals are granted the "legitimate authority" to make rules that *all other people* must follow and the "legitimate authority" to employ others to enforce those rules (violently if necessary), regardless of the reality that their rules violate the consent of countless peaceful people in nearly every instance.

If makes no difference if the people who choose the winner of the election *believe* the winner is granted special authorities. It makes no difference if the people who choose the loser of the election begrudgingly accept the same. Their beliefs have no bearing on the fact that all violations of consent are immoral.

While a general belief that elections grant extra authorities to politicians doesn't change the nature of violating consent, it *does* create a culture that ignores all but the most unspeakably egregious assaults on individual consent choices.

To suggest that any human being can be granted a new authority (one that is not already possessed by any other individual) by way of the "consent of the governed" is a complete misuse of the word "consent." It's a use that is offensive to the correct understanding of the word. It twists the fundamental principle that each individual has the sole authority to grant or withhold consent.

Respect for consent is the only basis by which a civilized society can survive. Society has survived thus far *in spite* of organizations attempting to shift the source of consent and morality from the individual to the organization itself. Religious organizations have been declaring themselves as the purveyors of morality for many centuries.

But there is another category of organization which has become the modern master of consent and morality. Recall the examples given the section on consenting for others. If I am able to consent for you, I can:

- Consent for some or all your property to be transferred to me

- Consent for you to hire me for my services at any price I wish

- Consent for you to take whatever medicines I decide

- Consent for you to give up your parental authority in your children

Today, these have more common names:

- Taxes, fines, and eminent domain

- Civil services and law enforcement

- Drug enforcement

- Child services

So long as humans remain human, self-ownership, agency, and the immorality of violating consent choices are immutable; they are inexorably connected to the human condition itself. No amount of vote-marking, self-declaration, group assertion, threats, intimidation, or violence will change that.

The government, through its legislation, declares which actions are "moral" and "immoral." They decide what actions are "bad" and therefore deserve punishment. And then they conveniently declare their own violent punishments to be "moral" — a blatant hypocrisy. When people suggest they know what is moral and immoral for everyone else, they are doing nothing less than telling others what they must consent to and from whom they must withhold their consent. Those who believe *their own* moral compass is what determines the rightness or wrongness of their actions (instead of correctly respecting the consent choices of others) are the cause of the vast majority of pain, suffering, and outright evil in the world.

The homeless and the billionaire revisited

In one of the moral dilemma examples, the scenario of taking property from one person in order to end an emergency for another person was explored. For some individuals, even if they strongly believe in the principle of respecting consent choices, it may be necessary to violate their own principle in order to rectify an immediate, life-threatening need. In that scenario, the one who committed the consent violation must still compensate the person they victimized while trying to solve the problem they felt was so pressing.

The hypothetical scenario of a child alone in a lake and an evil boat owner may never happen in reality. But every day there are thousands of people who could be considered in emergency need of food, medicine, and shelter while there are people with billions of dollars in resources at their disposal. If the violation of a boat owner's consent is justified to save a child's life, isn't the violation of a billionaire's consent justified in saving perhaps many lives?

Similar to the boat owner in the lake example, if the billionaire *truly had no part* in creating the situation the poor person is in, to forcefully take property from the billionaire is a violation of consent and therefore is an immoral act. Again, a peaceful human being is deserving of having their consent choices be respected, and there is no quantity of property that magically changes this. This is true despite the belief by some that the mere existence of a billion dollars under the control of a single individual is *prima facie* evidence of initiated harm against others. Such an assertion is factually untrue. Who would argue that George Lucas earned his wealth through aggression and exploitation? What about Oprah Winfrey, Michael Jordan, David Copperfield, or Paul McCartney? At the time of this writing, all of these people are billionaires who made their fortunes through a series of millions of individual voluntary transactions (ticket or album sales) or mutually beneficial contracts (such as product endorsements).

Even if it could be argued that the billionaire in question obtained his money illegitimately, it does not then follow that the money can be used for the benefit of those who were not *his specific* victims.

A society which allows non-victims to receive proceeds from victimizers is not a just society. This arrangement leaves the original victim without recourse or compensation for the crime perpetrated against them. It also creates a perverse incentive structure with one group of people asserting *they* should be doing the distribution (with all the corruption that task would inevitably create) and another group of people asserting they are deserving of the money regardless of *actual* need.

Consider also: The entire political class of Western civilization remains in power specifically because individuals such as police officers and military troops are willing to use violence against other human beings — not as individuals defending their own lives against a personal attack but *on the command* of those who won the elections. These enforcers have willfully given up their agency regarding their role in society. By forfeiting their agency, they have chosen to place the interests of their bosses *above* the consent of others. Perhaps if these individuals understood from an earlier age that no human has the legitimate authority to order the harming, imprisoning, or killing of others and thus refused to sign up for such positions in the first place, it wouldn't be possible for the elite to maintain the institutions by which they obtain their power and riches.

There are strong arguments that if not all, then most super-rich individuals directly benefit from institutions that are built entirely on violations of consent.

So what is to be done regarding those billionaires who actually do gain from immoral and criminal processes such as limited liability for oil polluters (thus making profits while their risks are subsidized by the public), access to the Federal Reserve for banks (thus using new money before its inflationary effects are seen throughout the economy), or intellectual property laws and trade limitations so companies can benefit from their enforcement (thus profiting from higher prices than would be possible without intervention)? These industries gain *real wealth* at the expense of *everyone else*. How are their victims — millions of individuals — to be compensated?

As unsatisfying as this answer is, there may be no immediate way to justly divide up the resources in these industries and distribute them equitably without the creation of another massively unjust organization (armed with guns and a willingness to use them) to do it. Such a method should be unacceptable to anyone who holds the fundamental principle of respecting consent.[48]

---

48 This is not to shy away from forcing those who are responsible for victimizing others from compensating who they owe; it is only to guard against *further* victimization in the process. To simply seize the assets of a large company by force will unquestionably create

Government exists *entirely* due to consent violations

There is no government act that does not originate with the violation of a peaceful person's consent. This fact deserves its own call-out:

> **There *is no act* any person in government can take that does not first require the violation of a peaceful person's consent.**

The reason for this is extremely simple: There is nothing any government organization owns that it has not first taken from others. A government does not make voluntary agreements with people in order to generate revenue. Every single resource it uses — to pay for government actors, to buy equipment, to create and enforce its rules, to exert its power — has been acquired via coercive acts. If a government agency sends you a letter, where did they get the paper and the envelope for it? They were purchased using money. Where did that come from? It came from a person who, if they refused to pay, would set off a chain reaction of events that would inevitably lead to physical violence being used against them.

Government organizations (to varying degrees) use the following methods to raise revenue:

- Fines and fees levied when individuals disobey the rules it invents

---

chaos and irreparable harm against many who do not deserve to be harmed. The creation of new victims in the pursuit of justice is the end of justice itself.

- The demand of payment on a timely basis of a percentage of earnings (income tax), a percentage of each private transaction (sales tax), or a percentage of owned property (property tax)

- The transfer of purchasing power from currency users (the public) to itself via means of debasement (printing new currency)

- Use fees on lands taken by force from others (or acquired by funds from the above coercive measures)[49]

- The borrowing of money with the promise to repay from income of the above methods

Government officials (politicians) get together and decide on a set of rules that dictate the total revenue people must give them. They then pass those rules on to bureaucrats in agencies who write up all the details, and in turn those updated rules are handed to enforcement groups who make sure everyone is obeying all the rules for providing revenue.

But this goes very far beyond simple extortion.[50] Individuals who consider themselves part of the government assert the legitimate power to control nearly every part of your life in some way. Consider the total number of rules

---

49 On occasion a government agency will solicit private donations to acquire property or pay for activities. These are the extreme minority of cases, but even then, they are managed by those whose salaries are drawn from the usual income measures.

50 For more insight into the crime of extortion search for the word "extortion" and compare it to the common concept of taxation.

that affect just making and selling a simple pencil. There are regulations on the extracting the raw materials (such as wood, graphite, clay, brass or aluminum, chemicals for paint, etc.). Transportation, labor, energy, packaging, selling, and even the very money used to buy equipment, parts, and supplies, all have their separate regulations and regulatory groups. There are tens, perhaps hundreds of thousands of rules that are imposed on you without your consent and without the consent of pencil manufacturers or sellers — rules that will be violently enforced at the discretion of government actors.

Government actors *do not care* about your consent choices. They have a very simple set of tasks: make rules for all others to follow and enforce them with threats of violence.[51] Due to this nature of government, we can safely conclude:

> **As a group, people who act in government positions are, without comparison, the single greatest violators of consent in the history of all mankind.**

If someone holds the idea that the violation of consent is immoral, then they *must also* hold the idea that the government is a wholly immoral organization. To believe otherwise is the greatest of all possible contradictions.

Those who claim "But the government protects us from___________!" or "The government provides us with___________!" (fill in the blanks) are

---

51 https://reason.com/video/raw-foods-raid-the-fight-for-t/

perfectly allowed to believe the price of violating the consent of peaceful people is worth whatever they think government is doing. Perhaps they believe there will be a net benefit to society. It is clear, however, that such a person simply does not believe the violation of consent is universally immoral. They have instead chosen some government provision that they personally view as more important than respecting the consent of their fellow human beings.

Ultimately, whatever product or service someone has put in the blanks above is completely arbitrary. It just happens to be the policy *they* want more than respecting consent. And there are always countless reasons given as to why___________ is so important we simply *must* use threats of violence in order to force people to pay for it, or participate in it, or stop doing it.

Take a moment and think back to the example of taking someone's boat to save a child's life. If some individual, say Rachel, was the one using *her agency*, and Rachel was the one *risking herself* against the chance others might (rightfully) decide to defend themselves against force, Rachel could at least argue that she felt it necessary in *that particular instance* to violate her own principle of respecting others' consent in order to halt a greater injustice.

If an individual is willing to risk what comes with violating a peaceful person's consent, then they will personally bear any physical, economic, and social damage that comes with their choice to act. But that is not how it works where government is involved. Individual government actors are almost never blamed[52] for their individual violations of consent as any ordinary (non-governmental) human being would be. When atrocities are committed, the individuals who actually perpetrated them are punished only in extremely rare cases. It's always "the government" that committed the atrocities, never specific people. Who starved millions of Ukrainians in the Holodomor?[53] Who murdered millions of educated people in Cambodia?[54] Who carried out the countless evils in World War I[55] and World War II?[56] Who committed the horrors against millions of Armenians?[57] Can you name the individuals who pulled the triggers or dropped the bombs? No one can name them because it was "government" that did these things. Government is the great whitewasher of crime. Out of the countless individual government actors who physically carried out these (and many other) crimes, only a tiny few have ever been held to account for their actions.[58] When the real people who *actually* commit these unspeakable acts can commit them in near anonymity, government becomes the greatest absolver of the worst criminals in history.

---

52 In the instances where government individuals are punished for their actions, it's rarely about violation of consent *per se*, but usually for a violation of their own policies.

53 https://holodomor.ca/

54 https://hmh.org/library/research/genocide-in-cambodia-guide/

55 https://encyclopedia.1914-1918-online.net/article/atrocities

56 https://time.com/3718981/tokyo-firebombing-1945/

57 https://www.armenian-genocide.org/

58 https://www.loc.gov/rr/frd/Military_Law/Nuremberg_trials.html

A Solution

Step one to a solution: Educate

As it stands today, there are very few people who recognize every violation of consent when they see it. Unfortunately, in Western society, most violations of consent are simply ignored or even considered "justice." This is because the lesson taught to nearly everyone from a very young age is that some individuals (e.g., those in the government) have the duty to violate consent on command. Therefore, the first step to ending widespread violations of consent is to educate others to start recognizing the practice and oppose it consistently.

Teaching people to see consent violations is much easier when the actions of individuals are examined for what they are, rather than who is committing them or by using euphemisms to describe them. Imagine the following scenario:

Your friend Julia invites you over to join her family for a holiday gathering, which you happily accept. Her family home is quite remote. When you get there, everyone seems genuinely happy and friendly. Everyone sits down to dinner where many fun stories of the family are told along with jokes and generally good discussion.

Just as a quiet moment in the conversation comes, you distinctly hear banging and someone yelling "Help!" from the basement. The family seems to hear it, but no one really gives it a second thought. You hear it again, and then again. Your curiosity gets the better of you. After sneaking away from the group, you follow the noise to the basement door and proceed down. To your amazement, you don't see a ghost but an actual, living human being who is locked in a cage built into the full basement of the house!

"Oh, thank god," he says, "Please get me out of here. I haven't hurt anyone or stolen anything! I didn't do anything wrong! I don't deserve to be here! Please!"

Just then, Julia comes in and calmly walks you back up the stairs, not bothered in the slightest that you have seen a man locked in her family's home.

Shocked, dismayed, and disgusted, you ask Julia why on Earth her family has a man locked in their basement.

Calmly, she explains, "That is my Uncle Joe. He is a member of our family. He is fed very well and given regular health care. You see, hundreds of years ago, the elders of my family made a decision: Each year, the leaders of the family make rules that all of us must follow in exchange for the benefits being a member of the family provides. Once a rule is written, it applies to each of us — our grandparents, our parents, us, and our children on into the future forever. We must all abide by the rules set by the leaders. Even if someone marries into the family, all *new members of the family must automatically abide by all the previous rules created throughout the years. Unfortunately, Uncle Joe didn't obey. He decorated his home with oleander — a very dangerous plant — and owning an oleander plant is strictly against the rules. So, in accordance with the rules, he was removed from his home and placed in this cage where he has to stay for two years. I mean, really, how else can we make sure people do the right thing if we don't punish them?"*

You come to the unmistakable conclusion that Julia and her family are dangerously delusional, and you immediately decide to take a ride share service home in case there's some unmentioned rule you must obey for receiving a meal.

Morally speaking, this scenario is no different from what happens every day in the United States. Julia's family in the story represents the government. They are the one group of people who create the rules other people must follow while also being the enforcers of the very rules they create. (In this example, the rule forbids the possession of a plant which is analogous to the U.S. federal government prohibition of substances it considers dangerous.[59]) It could be argued that the difference between Julia's family and a government is that a government is elected. But as mentioned, if an ordinary human being has no authority to jail someone for violating a rule they invented, there is no method by which they can authorize someone else to create rules and jail people for violating them.

---

59 https://www.dea.gov/drug-scheduling

Julia was unable to see that Joe's consent was being violated. She was so wrapped up in the belief that other people (her family's "elders") had the legitimate authority to bind human beings to their rules (including those not yet born) and in *her authority* to enforce those rules that it never occurred to her that Uncle Joe is, in fact, the victim of a heinous crime. This is how most people view the government. They are unable to see the ongoing violations of consent because they believe the government has legitimate authority to commit them. Only when one steps back and sees all humans on the same, self-owning level does it become clear which actions are made to truly further justice and which actions are simply crimes masquerading as justice.

Furthermore, no rule created before Joe was born can possibly have any bind on him. It is immoral to force a human being — under threat of caging or other physical violence — to follow rules they had no opportunity to even consider before being subjected to them. Even if Joe *explicitly consented* to being caged if he broke one of the family's rules, he is always free to withhold that consent because he is the only person with the legitimate authority over himself. If the family had been providing benefits to him for following their rules, then in response to Joe's decision to violate the rules, the family could withhold their consent to provide whatever benefits Joe may have been accruing. This is the nature of all mutually voluntary agreements.

Another educational opportunity is reducing or eliminating the culture of elevating those who use violence as the primary tool of their job. Violence must always be the *last and most unfortunate* act to take in order to stop an initiated aggression and avoided altogether if there is any other alternative. Raising the people whose very job it is to enforce arbitrary rules — violently if necessary — to the status of unassailable hero contributes to greater acceptance of violence in society.

Widespread knowledge of consent and morality is a necessary but not sufficient condition to bring about lasting peace.

Step two to a solution: Express

Once most members of society are able to recognize acts that violate consent, at least some of those people must be willing to express their disdain for them. While it can be argued for example that protests do not in and of themselves cause change, a mass of silent individuals most certainly won't.

A revisit to the equivalence principle can be helpful here. Imagine two individuals, Leon and Michelle, observing the same act at the same time, that of Oscar violating the consent of Nora, a peaceful person. Say for a moment that Leon believes Oscar, a government official, possesses a special authority over Nora and therefore *does not* believe a violation is even taking place, while Michelle recognizes the act as a clear violation of Nora's consent.

They both remain silent about the incident.

Is there any way, from the position of an external observer, to tell the difference between Leon's and Michelle's thoughts on the event? Does the fact that Michelle is completely correct on understanding the nature of the act (as she presumably learned in step one above) make any difference in the real world in terms of preventing future violations?

Opposing an atrocity and saying nothing is outwardly equivalent to supporting an atrocity and saying nothing.

Under no circumstance should this fact be misconstrued into suggesting that Michelle in this example should be *compelled* to speak. Again, coercing her to speak would be a violation of her consent if she chose not to speak. Silence *is not*, in fact, violence.[60] However, remaining silent does not contribute to a solution. If 99 out of 100 people knew that Oscar was violating Nora's consent yet kept eternally quiet, the violations would continue.

That people express their denouncement of violence and consent violations is yet another necessary but also insufficient condition for a permanent, long-term solution.

---

60 Silence and violence are nearly opposite concepts. Violence is an act. Silence is the absence of an act. The phrase "silence is violence" is Orwellian in nature and potentially destructive to a mutually respectful society. Actual initiated violence can be defended against by using the minimum amount of physical force necessary to halt it. If silence were truly equivalent to violence, then one could use the physical force necessary to end the silence. There are few concepts more antithetical to a peaceful society than the sanctioning of the use of violence to compel speech.

Step three to a solution: Effect

As long as human beings exist in the universe as human beings, there will always be those who wish to coerce, force, control, overpower, trick, rob, victimize, harm, and otherwise violate the consent of others.

No amount of knowing that they're being immoral will stop them. No amount of screaming in their face about how wrong they are will stop them.

Such people must be *physically* stopped. Bullies and thugs will do what they want until they are no longer allowed to continue. The logic and reasoning of self-ownership, understanding the source of our agency, and the knowledge that violations of consent are immoral give us only the foundation of *why* we can use force to halt aggressions, but we already know that thoughts and words are not actions.

Therefore, among the educated and expressive individuals mentioned in steps one and two, at least some of them must be willing to put these ideas *into effect*. They must be able to physically prevent or halt violations of consent by real-world assailants and do so while strictly following the principle of peace themselves by not creating new aggressions in the process. In a best-case scenario, no force at all would be needed, but there will always be times when people need to use physical force to defend themselves, their property, and the lives and property of others against aggression.

All three components — recognizing a consent violation when it is witnessed, speaking out against it, and halting it (peacefully if at all possible, or using the minimum amount of force when necessary) — must be strongly represented in society in order to begin the process of ending the systems built on the abuse of countless peaceful people.

Another Solution

Tell others about the importance of consent. Tell them where their authority over themselves comes from. Be respectful of others' consent choices and *truly* apply your respect for others' consent equally. Learn to recognize when actions are actually *aggressions* and not just actions you don't like. Assume you don't know what is right for others. Assume you can't even imagine what is right for them. Ignorant ideas aren't halted by insults, and they most definitely aren't halted by silencing them. If someone is forwarding an evil idea, refute it! Being better *makes you louder* without having to scream. You will rarely convince a bigot of their horrible ideas[61], but the lurkers on the margin will see the ideas of peace and the morality of mutually voluntary interaction when you speak. A cultural shift away from violence is a multi-generational effort, and we have very formidable opponents. *But it has happened!* Chattel slavery was an accepted institution for all of human written history. Now, only the most monstrous individuals would support it.

You *can* be part of the solution.

---

61 Do not ever believe it cannot be done, however. https://www.ted.com/talks/daryl_davis_why_i_as_a_black_man_attend_kkk_rallies

"Work may be your dominant thought, and
joy an afterthought. But joy is your true
purpose, and work the afterthought."

—Alan Cohen

Afterthoughts

As an interesting exercise, let's revisit the questions asked at the beginning of the book and see if your views on them are different than they were before. Or, at the very least, see if you can predict the answers based on reading this book:

1. Consider the situation where Ada violates the consent of Beth. Has Beth been wronged? *Why* has she been wronged?

    Answer: Yes, they have been wronged. Because every human being owns themselves and possesses agency, every human has the legitimate authority to give or withhold consent.

2. If someone takes an action that only affects themselves, could it ever be said they did not consent to their own action?

    Answer: No. The fact that a person *acts* (with the understanding they were not coerced) is a clear indication they consented to the act and its effects, even if those effects were later seen as undesirable.

3. Consider two random adults in the world who don't know each other. Can one of them give consent *for* the other?

    Answer: No. This was likely understood before reading the book.

4. Does the word "immoral" merely mean "unnatural," "disgusting," "indecent," "repugnant," "shameful," "scandalous," "loathsome," or otherwise "offensive to the sensibilities?"

    Answer: No. Often people *use* the word "immoral" to mean "I think that's wrong for a lot of reasons that have nothing to do with how other people may want to live a peaceful life, including an affront to my religion, or my belief in how people *should* live." In this sense they are using it to describe what they believe to be wrong, not what *others* have declared to be wrong based on their consent choices.

5. If a person truly consented to an activity or an action that affects them, can the person honestly believe that they are being immoral?

    Answer: Again, if people use the word "immoral" for "damaging society," then it's possible. When understanding morality in the context of consent, the answer is no.

6. Can a person both consent and withhold consent to the same act at the same time?

    Answer: No. The principle of non-contradiction states something cannot be X and not-X simultaneously.

7. Is it wrong to use the threat of violence against an otherwise peaceful person as motivation for them to act?

    Answer: Yes. Using a threat of violence against someone is coercion. Coercion against peaceful people is always a rejection of others' consent and is an aggression.

8. Should the morality of a particular action (if that action is right or wrong) be judged using the same method for anyone who does it, regardless of their job or intent?

    Answer: Yes. All human beings are equal in the necessity of having their consent choices respected. All human beings who intentionally violate a peaceful person's consent commit an aggression.

Additional Reading

Author's note: I do not agree with all the ideas in the following books, but I would be remiss if I did not offer additional material of interest.

No Treason: The Constitution of No Authority by Lysander Spooner[62]

Anatomy of the State by Murray N. Rothbard[63]

Democracy: The God That Failed by Hans-Hermann Hoppe[64]

Economics in One Lesson by Henry Hazlitt[65]

The Law by Frédéric Bastiat[66]

The Machinery of Freedom by David Friedman[67]

---

62 http://www.lysanderspooner.org/works

63 https://commons.wikimedia.org/wiki/File:Anatomy_of_the_State.pdf

64 https://mises.org/library/democracy-god-failed-1

65 https://fee.org/media/14946/economicsinonelesson.pdf

66 http://bastiat.org/en/the_law.html

67 http://daviddfriedman.com/The_Machinery_of_Freedom_.pdf